P9-CQT-073

Making & Painting Victorian Birdhouses

MAKING & PAINTING
Victorian Birdhouses

JOYCE RICE

NORTH LIGHT BOOKS
Cincinnati, Ohio

About the Author

Joyce Rice is a self-taught artist who loves drawing, painting and building one-of-a-kind projects. She began building and painting birdhouses about six years ago, and since then has won numerous ribbons and awards for her creations. Her birdhouses have been featured in local television programs and newspapers, and in an article in *Birds & Blooms* magazine. She regularly donates her birdhouses to charity auctions, where they are desired as collectibles.

Rice's passion for building unique projects is not limited to small-scale houses. She and her husband are building a new home that Rice helped design, wanting to make sure it was a house no one else had. Rice and her husband have five grown children. They lived previously in Eldridge, Iowa, and are building that new home in Lowden, Iowa.

Making & Painting Victorian Birdhouses. Copyright © 1999 by Joyce Rice. Manufactured in China. All rights reserved. The patterns and drawings in this book are for the personal use of the decorative painter. By permission of the author and publisher, they may be either hand-traced or photocopied to make single copies, but under no circumstances may they be resold or republished. It is permissible for the purchaser to paint the designs contained herein and sell them at fairs, bazaars and craft shows.

No other part of this book may be reproduced in any form or by any electronic or mechanical means including information storage and retrieval systems without permission in writing from the publisher, except by a reviewer, who may quote brief passages in a review. Published by North Light Books, an imprint of F&W Publications, Inc., 1507 Dana Avenue, Cincinnati, Ohio 45207. (800) 289-0963. First edition.

Other fine North Light Books are available from your local bookstore, art supply store or direct from the publisher.

03 02 01 00 99   5 4 3 2 1

Library of Congress Cataloging-in-Publication Data

Rice, Joyce.
    Making & painting Victorian birdhouses / Joyce Rice.—1st ed.
       p.   cm.
    Includes index.
    ISBN 0-89134-881-6 (pbk. : alk. paper)
    1. Painting. 2. Decoration and ornament—Victorian style. 3. Birdhouses. 4. Woodwork. I. Title.
TT385.R53   1999
745.7'23—dc21
                                            98-40475
                                          CIP

Edited by Jennifer Long
Production edited by Marilyn Daiker
Production coordinated by John Peavler
Designed by Angela Wilcox
Cover photography by Pam Monfort, birdhouses by Joyce Rice

For my husband, Jim, and my very large, wonderful family

who waited patiently for me to finish this book.

Thanks to Mark Mess, a wonderful photographer who showed me many times how to use a camera for the pictures in my book, and to Boyd-Fitzgerald, Inc. for the great job they did developing them. 🐦 Thanks to my friend Linda for giving me a hand. 🐦 Thanks to my neighbors, the Carmelite Nuns, who have followed the progress of my book and wished me well. 🐦 Last, but not least, thanks to God for giving me the talent and patience to create my birdhouses.

Table of Contents

Introduction

I've been an artist all my life. When I was a child, my family and I would sit around the kitchen table drawing pictures of the cartoon characters in the newspaper. My mother was a good artist and it was her way of keeping us entertained. My father was a wonderful carpenter who could build anything. Watching him gave me a love of making things with wood. As I became an adult, I found there was nothing I couldn't draw or make if I put my mind to it.

I started building birdhouses when an olive tree in my front yard died. I had planted the tree several years before and couldn't bear to see it go, so I had my husband trim all of the branches with his chain saw and I put a birdhouse at the end of each. That started the ball rolling for the unusual birdhouses I make.

Every birdhouse has its own story. I can usually remember where I saw the window or unique door that inspired me. They become very special to me by the time I'm done with them. I have given some of my birdhouses to charity auctions; the people that buy the houses often like them too much to put them outside. You may have the same attitude when you make your own birdhouses.

The birdhouses I will teach you to build in this book are very simple; they don't have porches or other difficult additions, and you don't need any previous knowledge of woodworking or carpentry to make them. What makes each one different is the style of windows, doors and flowers you paint on it. (In fact, you can adapt my painting techniques and patterns for use on unpainted, ready-made birdhouses.) It will be these painted elements that make people take a second look. I've often seen people staring at the curtained windows and trying to imagine what the house with the wonderful flower gardens looks like inside.

A word of warning goes with these birdhouses: If you start putting them in your yard, people will soon be coming to your door, wanting to take pictures and asking if you sell them. It will be your turn to take care of all the sightseers!

The birdhouses on my olive tree are starting to show some wear and tear. A coat of polyurethane would have helped them, but I kind of like the rustic look.

I am truly a lover of birds. From the first thing in the morning to the evening hours, I am graced with their wonderful songs and their antics as they play in my yard. I have watched many batches of baby birds be born here, and here they seem to stay. Most of the birdhouses in my yard are rustic, because I can build a dozen of them in a day. My birds aren't too particular—they just want a place of their own, out of the weather.

These are the first elaborate birdhouses I made. They've been through severe storms and winters, but the birds seem to love them the best.

Supplies for Building a Birdhouse

Wood

I use all kinds of wood. You can buy precut pieces at almost any lumber store. This saves time on cutting and sanding. I use a lot of ½" (1.3cm) plywood, good on one side. I use 1" (2.5cm) pine to cut out my chimneys. A ³⁄₁₆" (.5cm) dowel rod makes a perfect perch. New home construction sights are a good source for birdhouse lumber. The builders always have a large pile of throwaway lumber out front. It's best to ask first, but they usually don't mind if you go through the pile to retrieve pieces you can use. A lot of wonderful birdhouses can be made from what they throw away.

Drill

I use a ³⁄₁₆" (.5cm) drill bit to make the hole for the perch. For the birdhouses in this book, I used a 1⅜" (3.5cm) Forstner bit to drill the entrance holes. If you don't have this type of drill bit, use a spade bit or hole saw.

Saws

I use a table saw for cutting large pieces of wood and a scroll saw for smaller pieces like rooflines and chimneys. If you don't own either of these, scout out your neighborhood for a willing woodworker. Most building and home improvement centers will cut the wood you purchase from them to your specifications for a minimal fee. You can use a handsaw, but it will take a lot more work.

Nails

I use a pneumatic brad nailer, which runs off an air compressor, to assemble my birdhouses. This is an expensive investment if you don't already have one (mine was a birthday gift from my husband). Traditional hammer, nails and screws work fine; I used them for many years. Just be sure to fill the nail holes with wood filler before painting.

Wood Filler

Follow the manufacturer's instructions on your wood filler. Filling the nail holes and other surface indentations makes a nicer painting surface. After all, the birdhouse will be your canvas.

Sandpaper

I use fine sandpaper because it makes my painting surface very smooth. I sand everything by hand before I put the first coat of paint on, then sand again after the first coat of paint is dry. It's very important to sand the entrance hole because your paint job continues inside the hole as you'll see later.

Shingles

I use cedar shake shingles for my roofs. You can buy them at the lumber store, or check building sites, where they are being used, for throwaways. I also use 3M's Safety Walk. It can be bought in sixty-foot rolls that are 1″ (2.5cm) wide. It comes in black, brown and gray. It has a sticky back, but you will need to use some type of glue to make the shingles stick permanently.

Tracing and Graphite Paper

I've provided a pattern of each birdhouse featured in this book. You can enlarge these patterns on a photocopier to get them to the correct size, then use tracing paper to trace the drawing and graphite paper to transfer it to the raw boards and painted house. Use white graphite paper on dark surfaces and black graphite paper on light surfaces.

Ruler

You will need a ruler or straightedge to draw the lines for the clapboard siding and bricks and to check measurements when enlarging the patterns.

Painting and Finishing Supplies

Paints

I use acrylic paints. I have quite a collection of colors, but if you want to buy only the basic colors and mix them, you can achieve any color you want. If you can't find the exact color I've used, use the pictures to find a good match.

Brushes

I use a 1-inch or 2-inch (2.5cm or 5cm) bristle or sponge brush for painting the base coat on the house and applying the polyurethane. To paint the details, I use a no. 00 liner, ¾-inch (1.9cm) angular, no. 8 and no. 12 shader, and no. 1 and no. 6 round.

Sea Sponges

I use sea sponges to create some of my flowers. They can be found in any craft store, and I keep several on hand so I have a variety of clean surfaces available. I don't think you can achieve the same effect with a regular kitchen sponge.

Paper Plates

I use paper plates to dab excess paint from my brushes. They are also a good practice area for experimenting with sea sponges.

Spray Bottle

Keep one full of clean water to thin your paints.

Polyurethane

I use clear satin Varathane Diamond Finish. It has little odor, cleans up with water and dries in two hours.

Glue

Depending on what kind of roof you use and whether you plan on using the birdhouse indoors or outdoors, you can use a hot glue gun, Liquid Nails tube glue or a marine glue called PC-11.

Building a Birdhouse Step By Step

The following demonstration will show you how to build a basic birdhouse from start to finish. Every birdhouse in this book is built the same way. Any variations and all painting techniques are explained within the individual project instructions.

1 Making Templates

On a photocopier, enlarge the patterns for the house you want to build to the correct measurements. Trace the whole pattern onto tracing paper, then with black graphite paper, transfer only the outlines of each section to a piece of poster board. Cut out the basic shapes of the front and one side, creating templates. The front and back will always be the same, so you only need one template for both. You also only need one template for the sides. I use a $\frac{1}{2}'' \times 6'' \times 4''$ (1.3cm × 15.2cm × 10.2cm) poplar board throughout this book. Please note that it will only be $5\frac{1}{2}''$ (14cm) wide even though it will say on the board that it is 6" (15.2cm). If you purchase this type of board, you will only need to cut the rooflines and bottoms. Lay the template on your piece of wood and trace around it. You will need two sides and two front/back pieces.

2 Cutting the Pieces

Cut out the pieces with your saw. I use precut pieces of wood whenever I can because it cuts down on the sanding and sawing. Here I'm using a scroll saw.

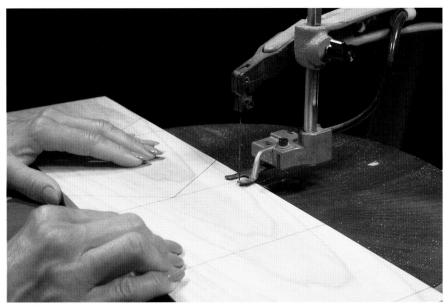

Basic Workshop Safety

- Wear eye protection when using saws, drills or any tool that produces dust and flying debris. Wear hearing protection when necessary.
- Don't wear loose clothing or jewelry that could get caught in machinery. Tie back long hair.
- Read, understand and follow all safety instructions included with all shop tools.
- Read, understand and follow all safety precautions provided on all chemicals (solvents, glues, finishes, paints and so on). Good ventilation is especially important when using finishes or glues with strong or harmful odors.
- Be sure to keep all of your tools properly maintained (sharp, clean, oiled).
- Don't work while you are tired or taking medication that might impair your judgment, and don't work too fast.
- Keep pets and children away from tools and solvents.

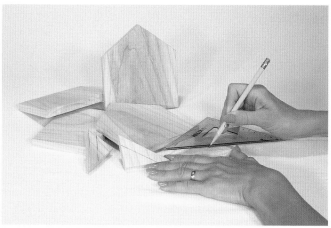

3 Cutting the Off Fall
Be sure to save those little corner pieces (called off fall) that come off the board after you have cut the roofline. We will be using them to beef up the area the roof will be nailed to. Draw a line across the piece of off fall to create a piece that is about ½″ (1.3cm) in width. This doesn't have to be perfect because it goes on the inside and is only for nailing purposes. Cut these pieces on your saw.

4 Marking the Holes
Cut out the individual pattern pieces from the complete tracings you did earlier, leaving 1″ (2.5cm) around the outside of the pattern. Position the tracing for the front of the house onto the front wood piece, holding it in place with artist tape. You only need to trace the entrance hole and perch hole for now.

5 Drilling the Entrance Hole
Cut out the bird entrance hole. I use a drill press with a 1⅜″ (3.5cm) Forstner bit for the entrance hole. A regular drill will also work.

6 Drilling the Perch Hole
I use my drill press with a ⅜″ (.9cm) drill bit for the perch hole. The perch will be attached after the entire house is painted.

7 Sanding
Use a piece of fine sandpaper to sand all of the pieces, including the inside of the entrance hole.

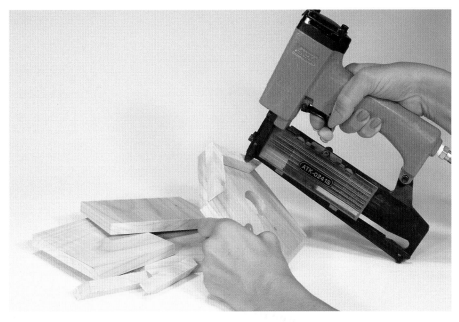

8 Attaching the Off Fall
On the back of the front and rear pieces, attach the off fall pieces you cut in step 3. Use a good, all-weather glue, then nail them into place at the roofline.

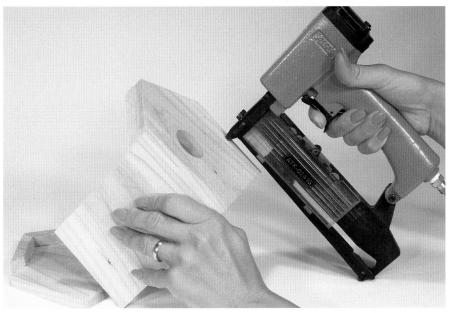

9 Assembling the Front and Sides
Attach the two sides to the front of the birdhouse with all-weather glue, then nails. Always attach the sides of the house to the back of the front piece, not to the edge of the front piece. If you attach them on the edge, the roof won't fit. Don't attach the back piece yet.

10 Making the Base
Use a piece of board called a one by six (2.5cm × 15.2cm) for the base. Lay the assembled front and sides on top of the board and trace the inside dimension of the birdhouse with a pencil. Use your saw to cut the base out. I always use scrap wood for the base of my birdhouses. You could use the same kind of board you used for your front and side pieces, but that's pretty nice wood to use on the bottom of a house.

11 Attaching the Base
Glue and nail the base inside the side and front pieces.

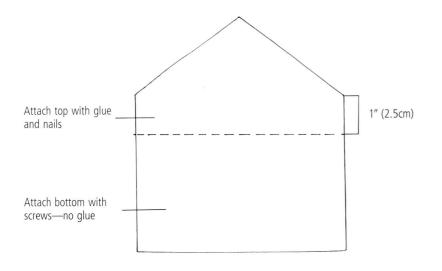

Attach top with glue and nails

1" (2.5cm)

Attach bottom with screws—no glue

12 Creating a Removable Back (Optional)

If you want to be able to remove the back of your birdhouse to clean it out, measure 1" (2.5cm) below the eaves on the back section and draw a line. Cut along this line with your saw, separating the "roof" from the bottom. Attach the bottom half of the back section to the sides with screws. Do not use glue. Next, attach the top of the back to the side pieces with glue and nails. It's easier to paint the birdhouse if you don't make the back removable; in this case, you can clean old nests out with needlenose pliers and a shop vac.

13 Attaching the Back

If you don't wish to remove the back, simply skip step 12.

Use an all-weather glue and then nail the back on.

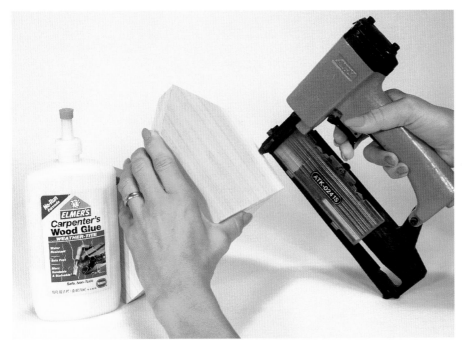

14 Filling the Nail Holes

Use wood putty, following the manufacturer's instructions, to fill the nail holes and any other indentations. I cut little pieces of poster board to apply my putty; they work just as well as a putty knife and can be thrown away when finished. When the putty is dry, sand it smooth with fine sandpaper. You are now ready to paint the house, following the directions for the project you have chosen.

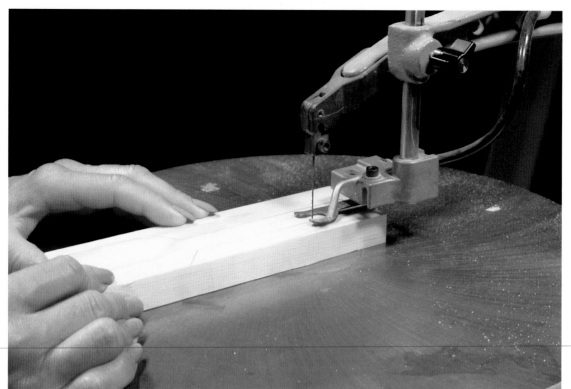

15 **Cutting Out a Chimney**

If your pattern calls for a chimney, cut a template as described earlier and trace it onto a 1″×3″ (2.5cm×7.6cm) piece of pine. Cut it out with your scroll saw or handsaw.

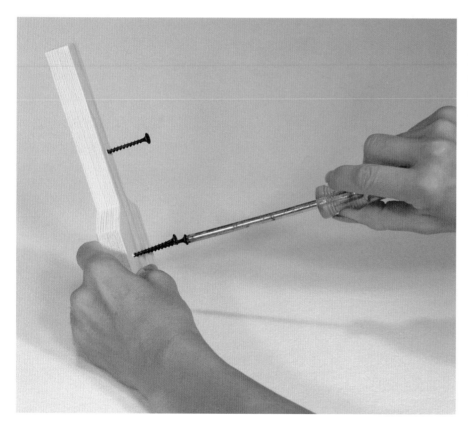

16 **Painting the Chimney**

Sand the chimney well, then barely anchor three screws in the back for it to stand on while the paint dries. Paint the chimney as directed in your project instructions.

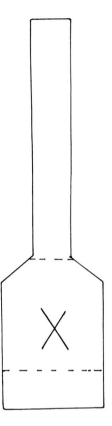

17 Attaching the Chimney

When the paint is dry, glue and nail the chimney to the back piece in the area marked with an X on the drawing. If you built a removable back, be sure you don't glue or nail the chimney in any other area, or it will permanently attach the back to the birdhouse. When you want to clean the birdhouse, remove the screws and grasp the chimney to pull the back off.

18 Attaching the Roof

Although the birdhouse in this picture is unpainted, you will be adding the roof after you've completed all of the painting and applied one to two coats of polyurethane. Make a template for one side of the roof, trace it onto a piece of ¼"(.6cm) plywood (good on one side), flip it over and trace it again for the other side of the roof. Write the word "inside" on the good side of each roof piece. Cut the roof pieces with a saw and sand them well, including the edge. Paint and seal the roof as directed in your project. The inside (painted side) will be the underside of your roof when the house is assembled. Cover the roofline with an all-weather glue and line up the cutouts on the roof with the chimney. Nail it in place. Shingle the roof as directed in your project.

Picture Collection

When I first started making my birdhouses, I used to make the windows and doors from my imagination. I still take some of my own ideas and combine them with some of the doors and windows I see. The United States is such a wonderful art gallery of windows and doors. Whenever I travel, I take my camera along and take pictures of buildings. Roaming around some of the older districts can give you a great source of window and door pictures. County courthouses, churches, old hospitals and general stores provide some of the most beautiful examples. I also take lots of pictures of stone buildings. By studying real stones or bricks, you will see how easy it is to paint them. To create the flower gardens for my birdhouses, I use my seed and plant catalogues and the flowers on my property for inspiration. I also keep a scrapbook of pictures of doors, windows and flowers that I have cut out of magazines.

Summer Cottage

Front

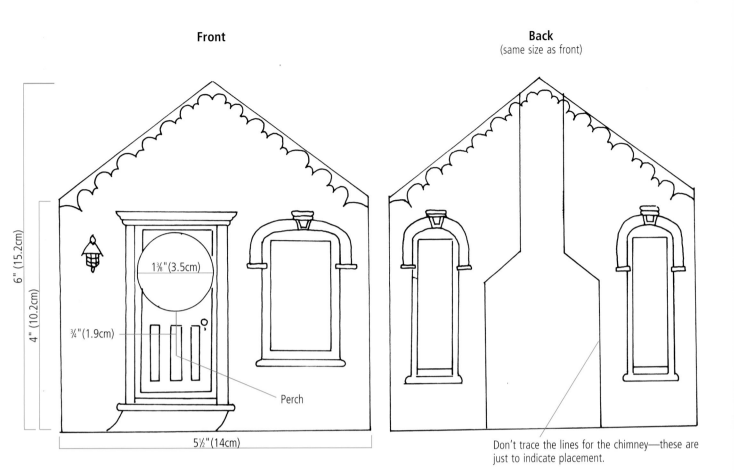

6" (15.2cm)

4" (10.2cm)

1⅜" (3.5cm)

¾" (1.9cm)

Perch

5½" (14cm)

Back
(same size as front)

Don't trace the lines for the chimney—these are just to indicate placement.

Roof
Cut 2 (a left and a right)

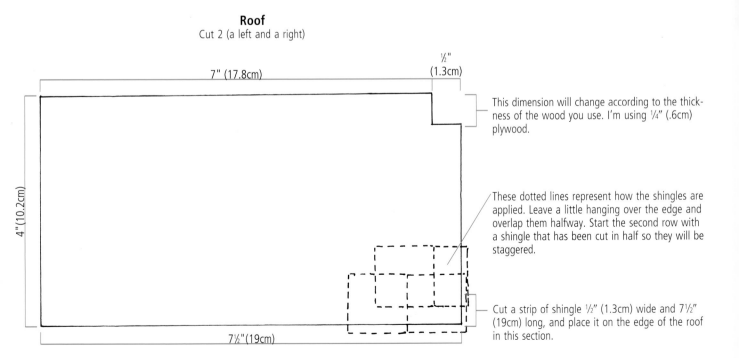

7" (17.8cm)

½"
(1.3cm)

This dimension will change according to the thickness of the wood you use. I'm using ¼" (.6cm) plywood.

These dotted lines represent how the shingles are applied. Leave a little hanging over the edge and overlap them halfway. Start the second row with a shingle that has been cut in half so they will be staggered.

Cut a strip of shingle ½" (1.3cm) wide and 7½" (19cm) long, and place it on the edge of the roof in this section.

4" (10.2cm)

7½" (19cm)

Enlarge patterns on photocopier 167 percent to return to full size.

Chimney
(cut from 1″ × 3″—2.5cm × 7.6cm—pine)

¾"(1.9cm)

4¾" (12.1cm)

2½" (6.4cm)

2" (5.1cm)

Sides
Cut 2

5½" (14cm)

4" (10.2cm)

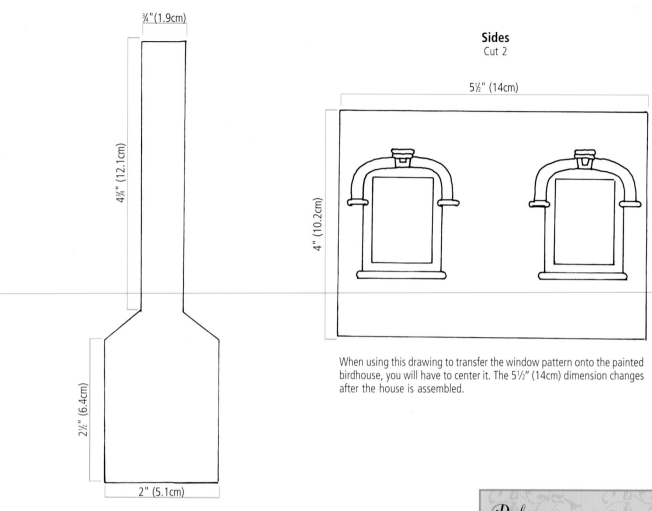

When using this drawing to transfer the window pattern onto the painted birdhouse, you will have to center it. The 5½" (14cm) dimension changes after the house is assembled.

Muntins
(trace these on after the windows are painted)

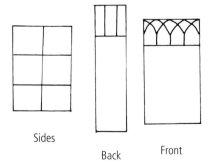

Sides

Back

Front

Enlarge patterns on photocopier 167 percent to return to full size.

Palette

Americana acrylic colors
• Hauser Light Green
• Midnite Green
• Mint Julep Green
• Neutral Grey
• Raw Umber
• Yellow Ochre

Apple Barrel acrylic colors
• Antique White
• Black
• Rose Bouquet
• Tapestry Wine
• White

Ceramcoat acrylic color
• Dark Brown

FolkArt acrylic color
• Linen

Flower colors of your choice

1 Building the Birdhouse

Using the patterns on pages 21 and 22, assemble the birdhouse as directed in steps 1 through 14 in the section on building a birdhouse step by step, or start with a ready-made birdhouse of roughly the same dimensions.

2 Basecoating

Basecoat the entire house with Folk-Art Linen, using a 1-inch or 2-inch (2.5cm or 5.1cm) sponge or bristle brush. When the first coat is dry, sand it smooth with very fine sandpaper, then add another coat of paint.

3 Transferring the Pattern

When the paint is completely dry, position one piece of the pattern on your birdhouse and tape it in place with art tape. Slide a piece of graphite paper beneath the pattern and lightly trace over the lines, omitting the panels in the doors and chimney. Repeat for all sides.

4 **Basecoating the Windows**
Outline all of the windows with a no. 00 liner brush and Black, then fill them in with a no. 8 or no. 12 shader. You will probably need two coats for opaque coverage. While you're using the Black, paint in the porch light with a no. 00 liner.

5 **Adding the First Trim Color**
Trim the windows, door and roofline with Neutral Grey on a no. 00 liner brush.

6 **Adding the Second Trim Color**
Add accents of Rose Bouquet as shown, again using a no. 00 liner brush.

7 **Adding the Third Trim Color**
With a no. 00 liner, add finer accents of Tapestry Wine as shown.

8 **Painting the Door and Window Frame**
Outline the door and paint the window frame with Yellow Ochre on a no. 00 liner, then fill in the door with a no. 8 shader.

9 **Finishing the Door Details**
Make an equal mixture of White and Neutral Grey to paint in the front walk. Fill in the rest of the porch light with White on a no. 00 liner. When the paint is dry, transfer the patterns for the porch light and door details. Paint the lines on the light, doorknob and lock with Black on a no. 00 liner, then thin some Black to a very watery consistency with your spray bottle and go over the remaining lines on the door.

10 Finishing the Trimwork

Repeat the previous steps for the sides and back of the birdhouse.

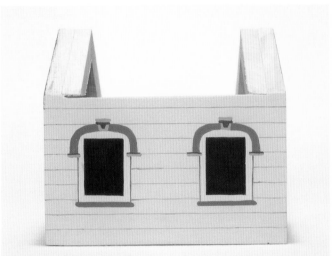

11 Adding the Clapboard

Using a pencil and straightedge, draw the lines for the clapboard siding ¾" (1.9cm) apart. It seems to work best to start measuring from the bottom and work up. Make a mixture of equal parts of Linen and Raw Umber, thinning it to a very watery consistency with your spray bottle. Use a no. 00 liner to follow the pencil lines very lightly.

 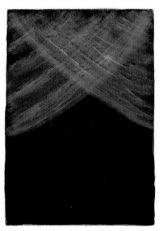  

12 Painting the Curtains

Paint a section of a paper plate black and allow it to dry. Squeeze a puddle of Antique White onto another paper plate and use the spray bottle to make it very watery. Pick up a small amount of the paint with a no. 6 round brush, then dab the bristles on a paper towel until they are almost dry. To see if you have too much paint on your brush each time you reload it, touch it first to the black area on your plate. In one sweeping motion, paint from one corner to the other. Let this side dry, then use the same technique to paint from the opposite corner. Add the bottom sections last. Don't go back over these strokes, or you won't achieve the effect of one sheer curtain laying over another. Last, transfer the muntin patterns from page 22 to your windows using white graphite paper. Paint these in with Antique White on a no. 00 liner.

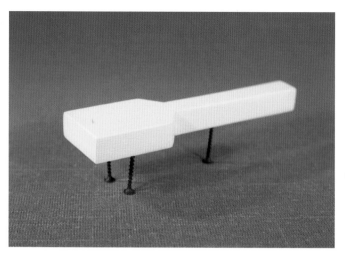

13 Basecoating the Chimney
Cut the chimney as described in steps 15 and 16 on page 18. Lightly attaching three screws to the back gives you something to hold on to while you basecoat, and they serve as "legs" for the piece while it dries. Basecoat the chimney with Antique White on a ¾-inch (1.9cm) angular brush, covering any part of the back that will show above the roofline. When dry, sand and apply a second coat. Remove the screws before you start the stone details.

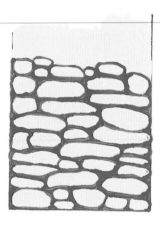

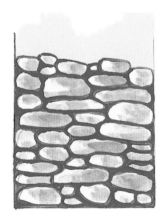
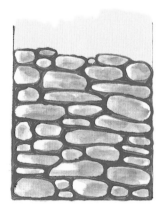
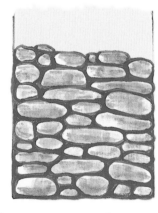

14 Adding the Stone Details
Draw the stones in with a pencil, covering the entire face of the chimney. Go over your pencil lines with Neutral Grey on a no. 00 liner. Fill in gaps between the stones and create a thicker outline around the stones with more Neutral Grey on your liner brush. This represents the mortar. Use your spray bottle to water down some Black. Pick up a very small amount on your no. 6 round brush and blot the bristles on a paper towel until you can barely see the paint. Lightly touch over random areas of the stones. You can practice this technique on an area of Antique White on your paper plate, as you did with the curtains. Do the same thing with Raw Umber, then with Dark Brown, allowing the paint to dry between each application. Using a slightly darker application of Black, add some shading in a few places. If you get any area too dark, immediately rub a damp paper towel over the area to lighten it. Paint a small area at the top of the chimney with Black to accent the opening. When the chimney is dry, nail it to the house in the area shown in step 17 on page 19.

15 Adding Shrubbery

There is no exact science to painting flowers and shrubs. No matter how many times you do it, they will never look exactly the same. The shrubbery is always added first. If you don't have all the colors of green I use, you can use a basic green, then mix three shades by adding Black, yellow or White. Use three different plates—one puddle of color per plate. Have a container of water handy to keep your sponges wet. Squeeze the excess water out of a sea sponge, then hold it in a towel until it is only slightly damp. Dip the sponge into the first color of paint and lightly dab it on an extra plate to practice making lots of tiny marks, then start on your house. Layer the colors as shown, allowing the paint to dry between applications.

Start with Midnite Green, sponging very lightly. Think of the sponge as nitroglycerin: If you give it more than a slight touch, it will explode into something you won't be happy with.

When the first color is dry, add Hauser Light Green on top of it, allowing areas of Midnite Green to show through.

Do the same thing with Mint Julep Green.

Finish the shrubs with another application of Midnite Green.

16 Adding Flowers

When you look at flowers against a house, you see splashes of color against a green background; you don't really see the individual details of the flower unless you get closer. Therefore, we will only be painting the *illusion* of flowers, not super-realistic blossoms. You can make these flowers with sponges or brushes. Using the techniques shown here, add flowers to the shrubbery all around your birdhouse.

Sponge Flowers

You can use any color you'd like for the flowers. I usually use a darker and lighter shade on each flower. You can load two colors on the sponge at once or apply one at a time. I use several sponges to produce lots of different marks. Experiment with various techniques and colors on an extra plate or piece of scrap paper.

Brush Flowers

I also use a no. 1 round and no. 00 liner brush for some of my flowers. The round is used for all of the dots and leaves, and the liner for stems and vines.

Brush Flowers

Sponge Flowers

To create clusters of blossoms like hydrangea and lilac, start with a darker color.

Allow the paint to dry, then add two lighter colors.

Pull the stems with one color of green on a liner brush.

Use the cut edge of the sponge to create tall, spiky blossoms—start with a dark color.

Then apply a lighter one.

Use the ruffled edges of the sponge to produce lots of single blossoms.

Dip a no. 1 round brush in a dark and light green. Start at the bottom and pull the leaves up, then down.

Make the dots with the round brush, connecting them as you go. Start small at the bottom and make them a little larger as you go up.

Use a darker shade to make tiny dots over the first color.

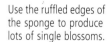

Load two colors on the leafy edge of a sea sponge.

Use a tiny corner to dab in centers for cone flowers or daisies with a darker color.

Use a leafy edge and a lighter color to create petals.

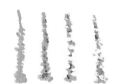

To make roses, load a no. 1 round brush with both a light and dark shade, then paint a circle. You can reload and swirl the brush as many times as needed until you're happy with the way it looks. Make the leaves with the same brush.

To make these flowers, lay a no. 1 round brush on its side to create the base dots, then continue up using less and less pressure on the brush to create smaller dots.

Connect dots made with a no. 1 round brush for the stalk. Add smaller, darker green dots. Use the same brush loaded with Antique White, laying it on its side for the blossoms. Shade the tips of the blossoms with the lighter green.

If you paint something you don't like, don't panic. I originally painted blue wisteria all over the front of this house and then hated it. (I do this all the time—it's called changing my mind.) Just tear off about a ¼" (.6cm) strip of very fine sandpaper, roll it up and sand off the stuff you don't like, trying to avoid as much of the other artwork as possible. Wipe the dust off and retouch the background. When it's dry, you can try a different flower.

Be sure and take the greenery around the side of the chimney. Use a no. 00 liner brush loaded with all three greens to lightly fill in the areas you can't reach with your sponge.

I made the daisies in the center with White loaded on a tiny edge of a fluffy sea sponge. When dry, I added a dot of Yellow Ochre to the center with a no. 00 liner. The stems are Hauser Light Green.

I made the leaves for the red flowers on the right by dipping a no. 1 round brush in Midnite Green and then Hauser Light Green, and using a smearing motion. Make sure your greenery ends up the same height where it meets at the corners of your house. At this time you can paint the bottom of the house a dark green color so it will gently blend into the greenery on the sides.

17 Making the Perch

Cut a 1¼″-long (3.2cm) piece of ³⁄₁₆″ (.5cm) dowel. If the hole you drilled previously is full of paint, clean it out with a ³⁄₁₆″ (.5cm) drill bit (holding it in your hand, not in the drill). Add a little drop of all-weather glue in the hole and drive the dowel in with a few light taps from a hammer or mallet. Give the dowel two coats of Yellow Ochre—the dowel is always painted the same color as the area it is located in.

18 Painting the Roof

Prepare the roof pieces as instructed on page 19. With Black acrylic, paint the edges, going slightly over the edge onto the outside, and 1½″ (3.8cm) from the edge on the inside of the roof. When dry, apply two coats of polyurethane, allowing it to dry between coats. If your piece will be displayed indoors, you only need one coat.

19 Varnishing the House

First, be sure to sign and date your house. This is your masterpiece and you want everyone to know it! Then apply two coats of polyurethane as you did with the roof. When this is dry, you're ready to attach the roof as directed on page 19.

20 Starting the Shingles

Refer to the roof pattern on page 21 for placement of the first few shingles. I will be using black Safety Walk by 3M. It comes in a 1″ (2.5cm) width, so I cut it into 1″ (2.5cm) squares for the shingles. For the first row, cut a strip of your roofing material that is ½″ (1.3cm) wide and 7½″ (19cm) long and use a hot glue gun to glue it to the bottom area shown on the pattern on page 21. When you start the second row, cut the first shingle in half in order to achieve the staggered look of shingles.

21 Completing the Top Row

When you get to the top row, trim the shingles off enough to make them fit. They should reach all the way to the peak of the roof.

22 Adding the Cap

I used red Safety Walk for the cap in this demonstration so you can see what I'm doing—you will use black. Cut the 1″ (2.5cm) pieces of Safety Walk in half and use hot glue to attach them as shown on the peak of the roof. Overlap each one. You now have a birdhouse you and your birds will enjoy for a long time.

The Little Country Church

Front

Back
(same size as front)

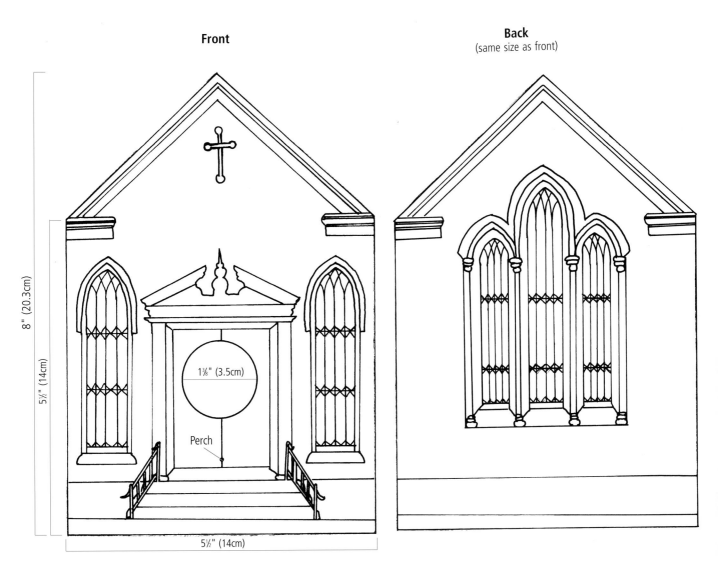

8" (20.3cm)

5½" (14cm)

1⅜" (3.5cm)

Perch

5½" (14cm)

Roof
Cut 2 from ¼" (.6cm) plywood

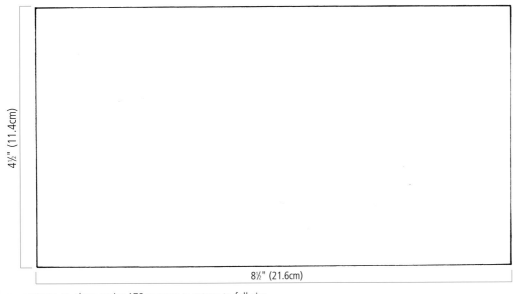

4½" (11.4cm)

8½" (21.6cm)

Enlarge patterns on photocopier 172 percent to return to full size.

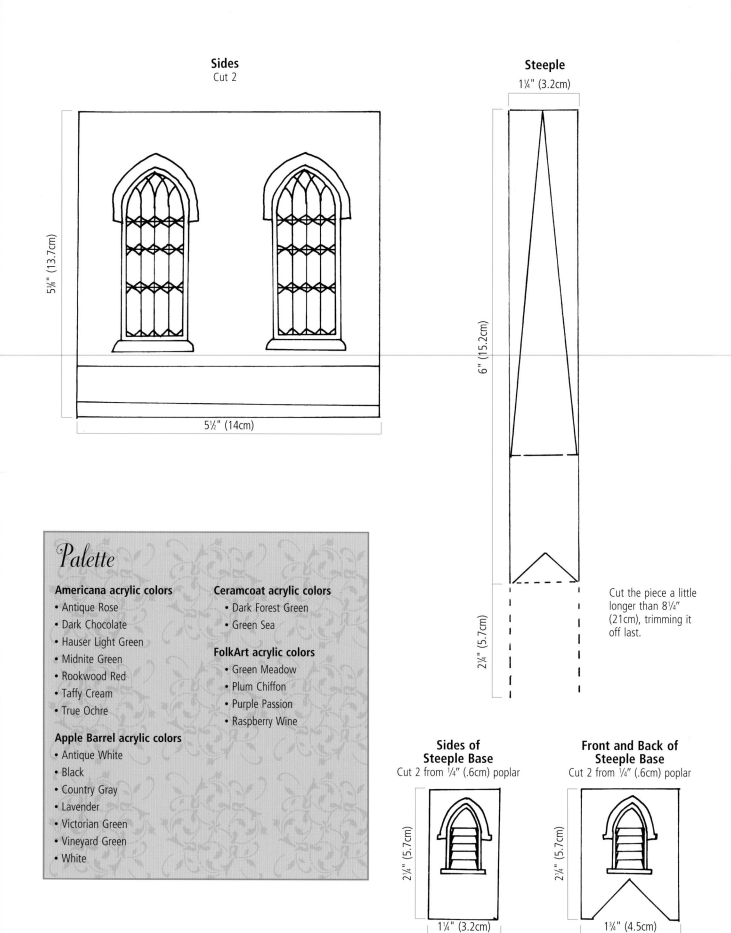

Sides
Cut 2

5³⁄₈" (13.7cm)

5½" (14cm)

Steeple

1¼" (3.2cm)

6" (15.2cm)

2¼" (5.7cm)

Cut the piece a little longer than 8¼" (21cm), trimming it off last.

Palette

Americana acrylic colors
• Antique Rose
• Dark Chocolate
• Hauser Light Green
• Midnite Green
• Rookwood Red
• Taffy Cream
• True Ochre

Apple Barrel acrylic colors
• Antique White
• Black
• Country Gray
• Lavender
• Victorian Green
• Vineyard Green
• White

Ceramcoat acrylic colors
• Dark Forest Green
• Green Sea

FolkArt acrylic colors
• Green Meadow
• Plum Chiffon
• Purple Passion
• Raspberry Wine

Sides of Steeple Base
Cut 2 from ¼" (.6cm) poplar

2¼" (5.7cm)

1¼" (3.2cm)

Front and Back of Steeple Base
Cut 2 from ¼" (.6cm) poplar

2¼" (5.7cm)

1¾" (4.5cm)

Enlarge patterns on photocopier 172 percent to return to full size.

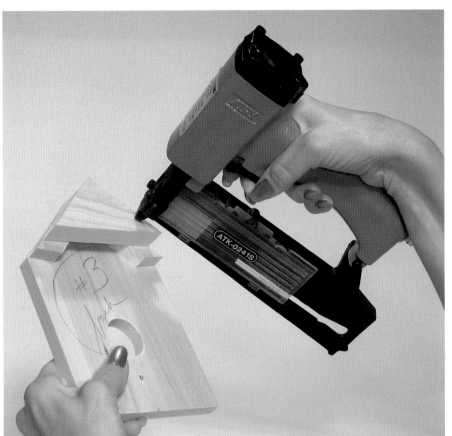

1 Building the Birdhouse

The Little Country Church uses the same basic design as the Summer Cottage. You will again use 5½"-wide (14cm) poplar board, and the entrance and perch holes are the same size. The only difference is the church is a little taller. Use the patterns from pages 33 and 34 to cut out all the pieces, then follow the directions on pages 13–17 to build the birdhouse. After nailing the off fall pieces to the inside of the front and back pieces, nail a piece of scrap one-by pine over the off fall on the front piece to beef up the area where the steeple will be attached. One-by is a generic term for the thickness of a 1" (2.5cm) board which is really only ¾" (1.9cm) thick.

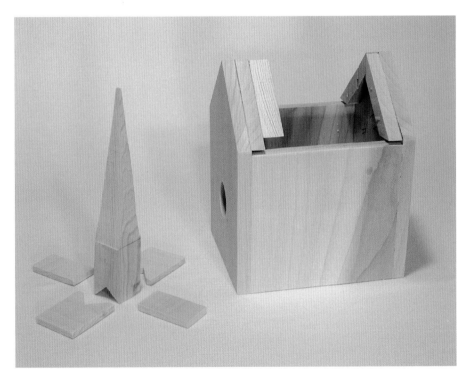

2 Making the Steeple

I am using a piece of scrap 1¼"-thick (3.2cm) pine. You could also use a piece of 2"×2" (5.1cm×5.1cm) pine, cut down to 1¼" (3.2cm) or left as is, which will give you a true 1½" (3.8cm) dimension. (If you choose not to cut the pine down, you will need to add ¼" (.6cm) to both the base and pointed parts of the pattern.) Transfer the lines to your wood for the front of the steeple, then trace the lines again on one side of the steeple. Saw along the lines on the front, then tape the pieces tightly together exactly as they were. Now saw along the lines on the side. The 6" (15.2cm) dimension isn't critical—if you have too sharp of a point at the top, take the very tip off. To cut a perfect steeple you really need expensive cutting tools. Since we'll be covering any imperfections in our steeple with shingles, we can use a simple scroll saw or handsaw to cut the steeple. Next cut out the V shape at the base of the steeple. Sand all of the pieces of the steeple, then glue and nail the base pieces onto the steeple as they are positioned in this picture.

3 Basecoating and Stonework

Fill the nail holes in the church and steeple with wood filler and sand them when dry. Basecoat both with Antique White. You don't need to paint the pointed part of the steeple as it will be shingled over. When dry, transfer the windows, door and other details with black graphite paper. Basecoat the door trim, eave trim, window trim and stone areas with very watery Dark Chocolate. When dry, draw in the stones with a pencil. Use thicker Dark Chocolate for the mortar between the stones. Last, shade the stones with a little watery Black.

4 Trimming Windows

To paint the darker areas on the window trimwork, start with a very watery Dark Chocolate and gradually build up layers until you reach the darkness you desire.

Watery Dark Chocolate

Pencil in stones

Dark Chocolate for mortar

Shade with Black

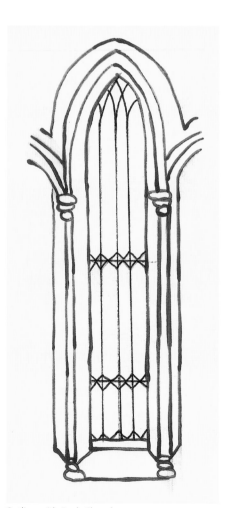

Outline with Dark Chocolate

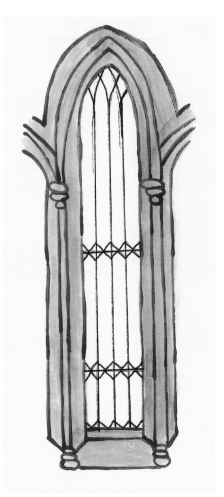

Fill in with watery Dark Chocolate

Build up dark areas with layers of Dark Chocolate

Outline in Dark Chocolate

Fill in trim with Dark Chocolate

Go over louvers with watery Dark Chocolate

Detail with Black

5 Painting the Steeple Louvers

When you paint the louvered windows on the steeple, be sure to add the little black triangles that make the louvers stand out. I've demonstrated a few of these around the final step.

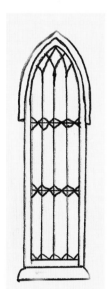

Transfer details

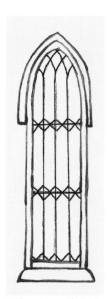

Outline trim with Dark Chocolate

Fill in trim with Dark Chocolate

Go over lead lines with Black

6 Painting the Stained Glass Windows

Next paint the lead lines in the windows and the railings on the steps Black. We will paint the windows with Dark Forest Green, using the same technique as used in step 12 in the first project to paint the curtains. Water the color down, blot your brush on a napkin and apply one coat. When dry, go back over some areas to make them a little darker. You can practice this effect on a paper plate painted with Antique White. Use the same technique to paint the remaining panes with True Ochre and Rookwood Red as shown. Although I'm only using three colors on my windows, you may decide to paint each section of the windows with different colors. If you're not happy with something you've painted, paint over it with Antique White, allow it to dry and start again.

Wash in watery Dark Forest Green

Darken some areas

Add Rookwood Red

Add True Ochre

7 Adding the Details

Using a pencil and straightedge, draw the lines for the clapboard siding ¾" (1.9cm) apart. Use a no. 00 liner to follow the pencil lines very lightly with a watery mixture of Dark Chocolate. Paint the front door and cross with Rookwood Red. Paint in the lines on the front steps with Black, then fill in the steps and sidewalk with Country Gray. Add Green Meadow to the bottom of the church under the stone and paint the base of the church as well. Paint the perch with Country Gray.

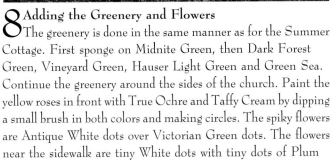

8 Adding the Greenery and Flowers

The greenery is done in the same manner as for the Summer Cottage. First sponge on Midnite Green, then Dark Forest Green, Vineyard Green, Hauser Light Green and Green Sea. Continue the greenery around the sides of the church. Paint the yellow roses in front with True Ochre and Taffy Cream by dipping a small brush in both colors and making circles. The spiky flowers are Antique White dots over Victorian Green dots. The flowers near the sidewalk are tiny White dots with tiny dots of Plum Chiffon in the centers. The dark roses on the back are Rookwood Red and Antique Rose. The roses on the right are Antique Rose and Taffy Cream. The yellow flowers on the back are dots of True Ochre and Taffy Cream, loaded on the brush at the same time. Use combinations of Lavender then Purple Passion, and Antique Rose loaded with Rookwood Red for the side flowers. Add leaves with a small brush loaded with a dark and light green at the same time. Be sure to sign and date your church.

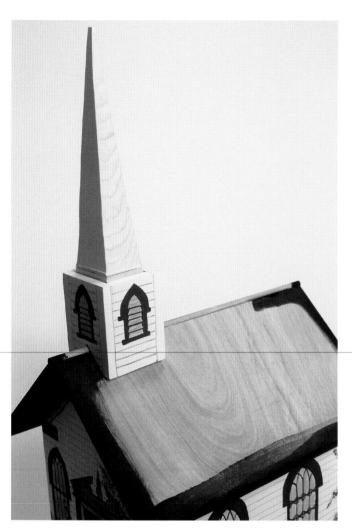

9 Attaching the Roof and Steeple

Paint the underside of the roof pieces with Black. Polyurethane the entire church, the base of the steeple and the underside of the roof pieces. Use two coats if your church will be hung outdoors. Use an all-weather glue to attach the roof to the church. I added a ³⁄₁₆″ (.5cm) dowel rod at the peak and painted the ends Black after gluing it in place. Use all-weather glue to secure the steeple onto the roof, then nail it in place.

10 Shingling the Steeple

I used black Safety Walk, which comes in 1″-wide (2.5cm) strips. Cut a strip 4½″ (11.4cm) long, cut it in half, then cut each of the pieces in half the long way. You should have four pieces 2¼″ (5.7cm) long and ½″ (1.3cm) wide. These go on the top edge of the base of the steeple; glue the first two pieces opposite each other. Cut the ends of the second pieces at an angle and glue them opposite each other, with their ends overlapping the first set. Now lay a strip of 1″-wide (2.5cm) shingle on the first side of the steeple. Cut it to the proper angle and glue it in place. Glue the second shingle halfway up from the first and trim to size, then continue up, gluing a shingle every half inch. You can complete one side at a time or work each row around the entire steeple. When you've covered the entire steeple, cut four long strips to glue vertically over the four edges.

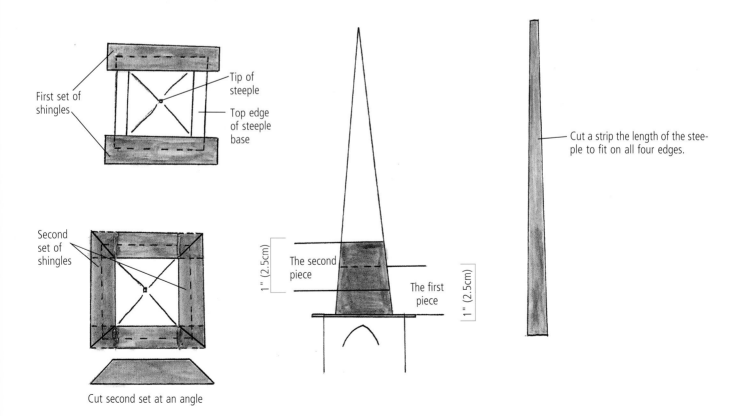

First set of shingles

Tip of steeple

Top edge of steeple base

Second set of shingles

Cut second set at an angle

1″ (2.5cm)

The second piece

The first piece

1″ (2.5cm)

Cut a strip the length of the steeple to fit on all four edges.

11 Shingling the Roof

Cut the Safety Walk in 1″ (2.5cm) squares to shingle the roof. Put down a long strip along the bottom of the roof, then hot glue the shingles as in the previous project. I used a long strip of Safety Walk along the peak, rather than little pieces. This is just another option available to you. You could also paint the roof and steeple if you don't want to shingle it—Safety Walk can get a little pricey.

White Townhouse
With Gray Shingles

Back

Front
(same size as back)

13" (33cm)

8½" (21.6cm)

5½" (14cm)

1¼"
(3.2cm)

Perch

1¼"
(3.2cm)

Perch

Line up the bottom of the inside shelf for the second
story here if you will be creating a removable back.

Enlarge patterns on photocopier 168 percent to return to full size.

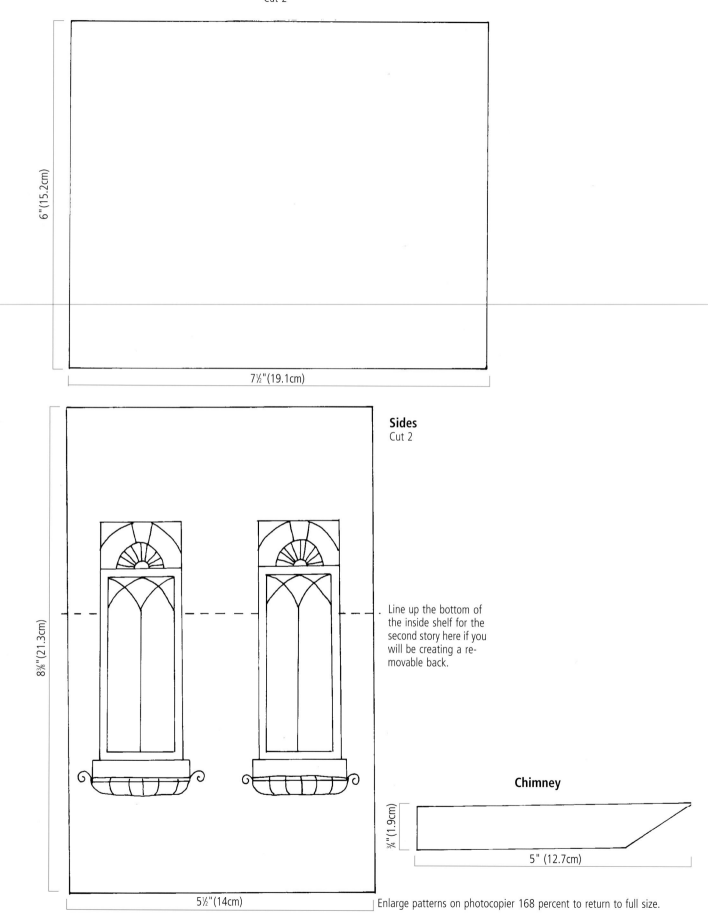

Roof
Cut 2

6"(15.2cm)

7½"(19.1cm)

Sides
Cut 2

Line up the bottom of the inside shelf for the second story here if you will be creating a re-movable back.

8⅜"(21.3cm)

5½"(14cm)

Chimney

¾"(1.9cm)

5" (12.7cm)

Enlarge patterns on photocopier 168 percent to return to full size.

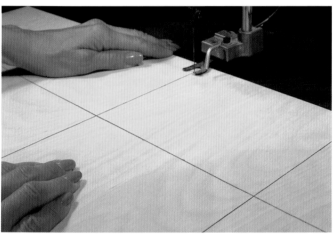

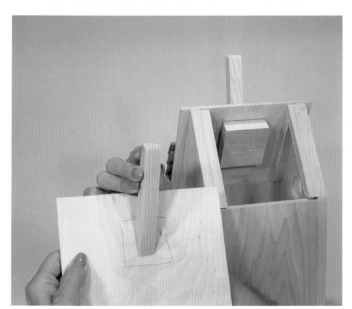

1 Adding the Second Story

The townhouse is cut out and assembled in the same way as the previous houses. The only differences are that you will be adding a shelf inside to create a second story, and using a 1¼" (3.2cm) spade or Forstner bit for the entrance hole. (The perch hole remains the same diameter.) The next three townhouses are built in exactly the same way as this one.

Using 6" (15.2cm) precut poplar board, which is actually 5½" (14cm) wide, cut all the pieces you need. From a scrap of one-by pine, cut another piece the same size as your base; this will be used to divide the birdhouse into two compartments. Assemble the front, sides and base. If you want to remove the back for cleaning, you will need to line the bottom of the second-story shelf up with the dotted line on the pattern. If you won't be removing the back, you can move the shelf up or down as desired. Use an all-weather glue to position the shelf inside the house, then secure it with nails. Attach the back, skipping the glue if you will be removing it for cleaning.

2 Cutting the Roof and Chimney

We will be cutting out the roof pieces now because there will be some painting you will want to do before assembling them; the chimney will also have to be painted before you attach it to the roof. Remember, the roof won't be attached until all of the painting on the house is finished. Cut two roof pieces from ¼"-thick (.6cm) plywood. I buy a piece of plywood that is 12" (30.5cm) wide so that all I have to do is draw lines on it and cut it with my scroll saw. Use the good side for the underside that gets the paint. Cut the chimney from a piece of ¾" (1.9cm) stock pine or one-by pine.

3 Beefing Up the Roof

At this time, cut a 2"-square (5.1cm) piece of scrap one-by pine—this will beef up the roof where the chimney will be nailed later. Glue and nail the block to the inside of the roof piece. *Do not* attach the roof pieces or chimney until after you've painted the house. (I've temporarily assembled them in this picture just to show you how it will work.) On the outside of the roof, mark the area where you've added the 2" (5.1cm) block. Once you nail the roof on, you won't be able to see the block. *Note*: You will only add one chimney—I've shown two here to demonstrate how the chimney is attached from both the inside and outside view.

12 Finishing the Chimney

Paint the chimney with two coats of White, sanding between coats. Using a pencil and straightedge, divide the chimney into horizontal lines, each ¼" (.6cm) apart. Paint over the lines with Neutral Grey. Stagger the vertical lines to represent bricks. Use Neutral Grey to thicken the mortar lines and create little triangles at the top and bottom of each vertical line. Last, shade random bricks with very watery Neutral Grey. When dry, give the chimney two coats of polyurethane. Paint the underside of the roof pieces with Neutral Grey and polyurethane, and nail and glue in place. Nail the completed chimney to the roof in the marked area.

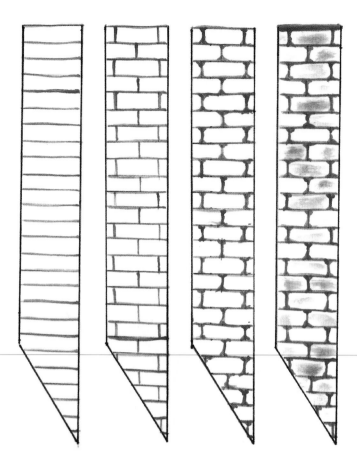

13 Adding the Shingles

Cut a ⅜″ (1cm) dowel the length of the roof peak. Paint only the ends with Neutral Grey. When dry, glue it into the valley of the roof peak. Cut a ½″-wide (1.3cm) strip of gray Safety Walk for the bottom edge of the roof. Hot glue in place, then work up to about the middle of the dowel rod with 1″ (2.5cm) shingles, as in the previous projects. Trim the shingles to fit around the chimney.

14 Capping the Roof

The last thing you will have to do is put a cap on the roof. Cut eight pieces of Safety Walk into 1½″ (3.8cm) lengths. Glue them in place over the dowel lengthwise, end-to-end; you won't need to overlap when using a dowel rod. (Note that I've finally added the doorknob!)

PROJECT 4

Yellow Townhouse
With Black Shingles

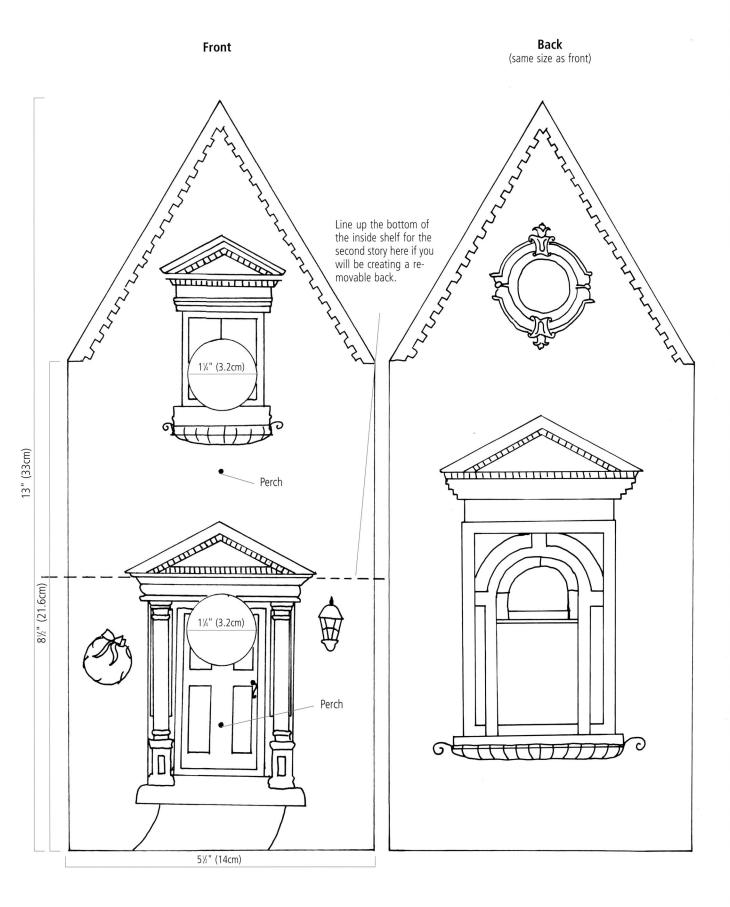

Front

Back
(same size as front)

13" (33cm)

8½" (21.6cm)

1¼" (3.2cm)

Line up the bottom of the inside shelf for the second story here if you will be creating a re-movable back.

Perch

1¼" (3.2cm)

Perch

5½" (14cm)

Enlarge patterns on photocopier 167 percent to return to full size.

Sides
Cut 2

Chimney

¾" (1.9cm)

5" (12.7cm)

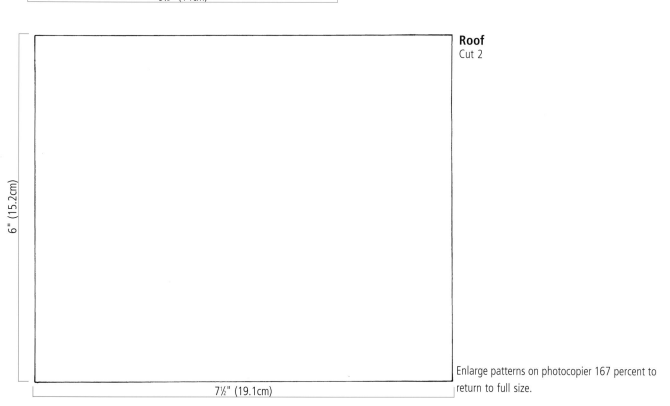

8⅞" (21.3cm)

Line up the bottom of the inside shelf for the second story here if you will be creating a removable back.

5½" (14cm)

Roof
Cut 2

6" (15.2cm)

7½" (19.1cm)

Enlarge patterns on photocopier 167 percent to return to full size.

1 Basecoating

Follow the instructions for cutting and assembling the townhouse given in the previous project, again cutting the pieces from 5½"-wide (14cm) poplar board and making the entrance holes 1¼" (3.2cm). Putty and sand the assembled house. Paint a basecoat of Lemon Chiffon, let it dry and sand with very fine sandpaper. Then put on the second coat of Lemon Chiffon. Transfer the design with black graphite paper.

Palette

Apple Barrel acrylic colors
- Antique White
- Black
- Country Gray
- Forest Green
- Leaf Green
- Lemon Chiffon

Ceramcoat acrylic color
- Antique Gold

FolkArt acrylic colors
- Camel
- Clover
- English Mustard
- Grape Juice (substitute Folk-Art Purple Passion or Red Violet if you don't have this color)
- Plum Chiffon

Flower colors of your choice

Front Door

Grape Juice

Antique Gold

Thick Black for details, watery Black for lines

Plum Chiffon

Large Back Window

Black

Grape Juice

Antique Gold

Plum Chiffon

2 Painting the Door and Back Window

Fill in the window with Black. Start the trimwork with Grape Juice. Paint in the door and other trimwork with Antique Gold. Use black graphite paper to transfer the lines over the door. Fill in the porch light, sidelight windows (they just peek out from either side of the columns) and doorknob with Black. Water down the Black to paint over the door lines. Use white graphite paper to transfer the details over the windows and doors. Paint them with Plum Chiffon.

Small Back Window

Black

Grape Juice

Antique Gold

Watery Black details

Plum Chiffon

Front Window

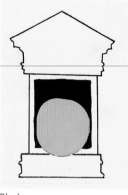

Black

Grape Juice

Antique Gold

Plum Chiffon

Side Windows

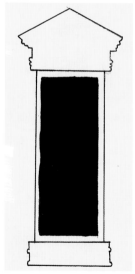

Black

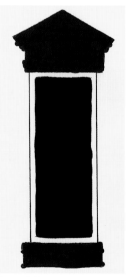

Grape Juice

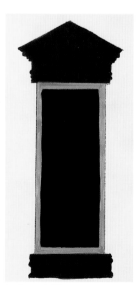

Antique Gold

Plum Chiffon

3 **Painting the Remaining Windows**
Paint the small back window and the windows on the side and front in the same way you did for the large back window: fill in the window with Black, start the trim with Grape Juice, then Antique Gold. Transfer the detail lines and paint over them with Plum Chiffon. Now paint all of the curtains in with watery Antique White. When dry, transfer the muntin lines with white graphite paper and paint them with Antique White, making sure to carry the lines inside the entrance holes.

Flower Baskets

Wreath

4 **Painting the Flowers and Greenery**
Using black graphite paper, transfer the window flower baskets and the circle for the wreath. Paint the baskets with Black paint, then fill them in with Camel. Remember, the Camel doesn't have to be perfect as it will mostly be covered up with flowers and greenery. To paint the greenery in the flower baskets and around the house, sponge in Forest Green first, then Clover, then Leaf Green and finish with a smidge of Forest Green again. Paint the bottom of the house a dark green. Now sponge in the purple flowers using various purples; I used Plum, Black Plum and Orchid (all from Americana), Apple Barrel Lilac Dust and then more Plum. Sponge a little greenery over the wreath circle. Using a no. 1 round brush, make tiny white circles, then add a slight touch of purple. Paint in the bow and ribbon with the color of your choice—I used Black Plum.

5 **Finishing the Townhouse**
Using a pencil and straightedge, draw in the lines for the clapboard siding ³⁄₁₆″ (.5cm) apart. Paint over the lines with very watery Antique Gold. Paint the step and sidewalk as you did for the previous project. Next add the perches; the top one is painted Lemon Chiffon and the lower one is Antique Gold. Sign and date the house, then give it one to two coats of polyurethane. While this is drying, cut out the chimney and paint it, following the instructions from the previous project but basecoating with Grape Juice and filling the mortar in with English Mustard. Shade the bricks with watery white. When dry, polyurethane the chimney. Paint the underside of the roof Black.

Glue and nail the roof in place with all-weather glue, then glue and nail the chimney to the area where you've attached the scrap block underneath. I again used black Safety Walk for the shingles. To show another roofing variation, this time I used scrap pieces of shingle that are all different sizes. I also trimmed the shingles for the peak with a radius on the edge and omitted the dowel rod. Otherwise, the shingles are applied in the same manner as in previous projects.

Red Brick Townhouse With Cedar Roof

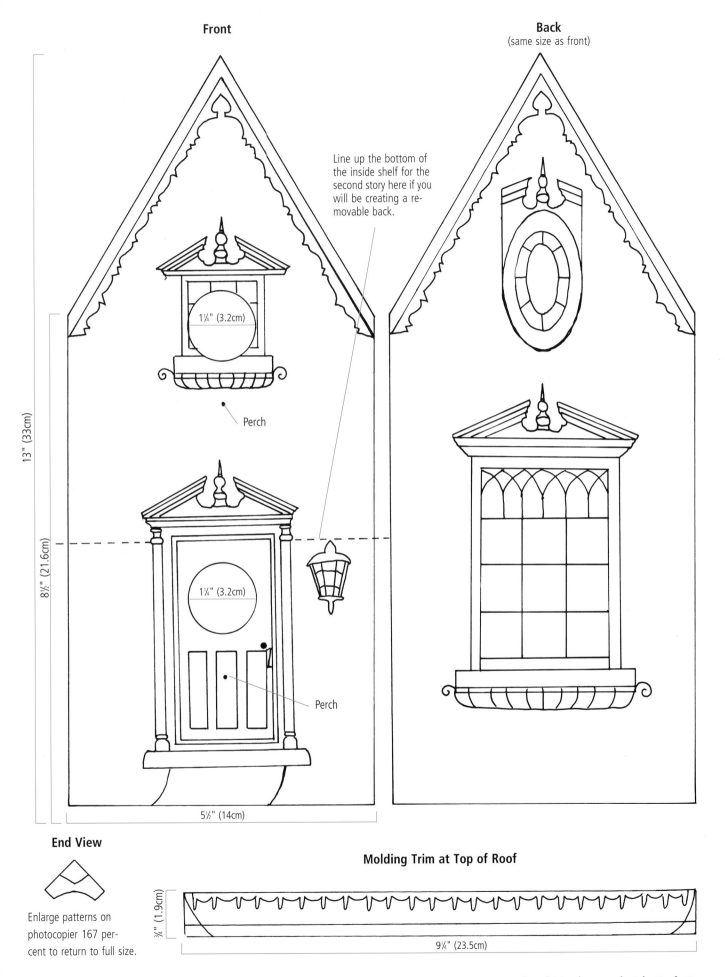

Front

Back
(same size as front)

Line up the bottom of the inside shelf for the second story here if you will be creating a re-movable back.

1¼" (3.2cm)

Perch

13" (33cm)

8½" (21.6cm)

1¼" (3.2cm)

Perch

5½" (14cm)

End View

Enlarge patterns on photocopier 167 percent to return to full size.

Molding Trim at Top of Roof

¾" (1.9cm)

9¼" (23.5cm)

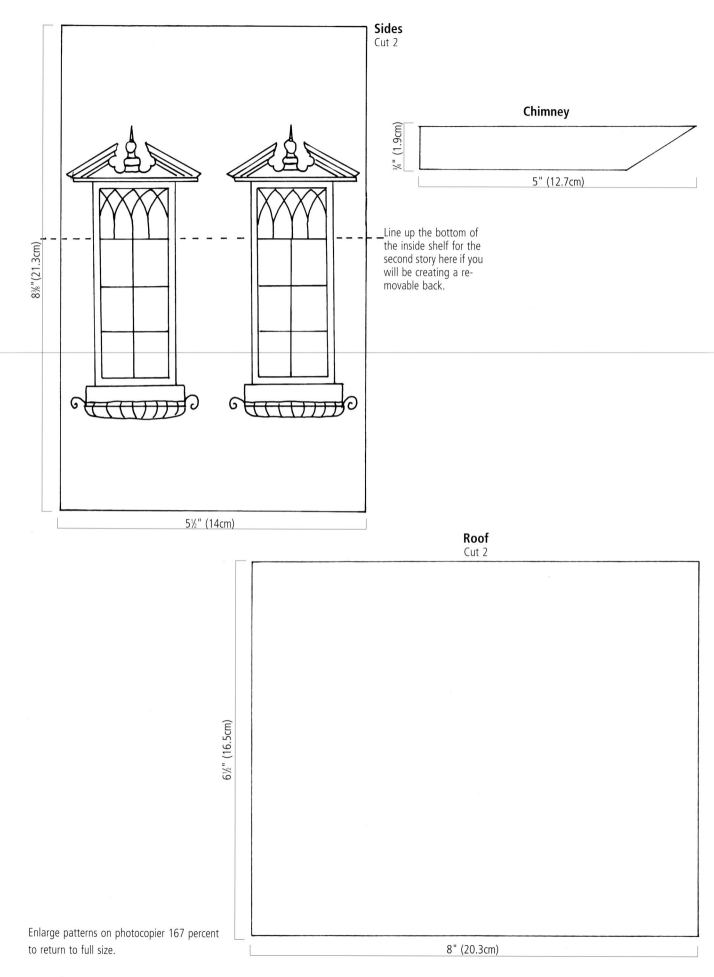

Sides
Cut 2

Chimney

¾" (1.9cm)

5" (12.7cm)

8⅜"(21.3cm)

Line up the bottom of the inside shelf for the second story here if you will be creating a re-movable back.

5½" (14cm)

Roof
Cut 2

6½" (16.5cm)

Enlarge patterns on photocopier 167 percent to return to full size.

8" (20.3cm)

1 Basecoating

Follow the instructions for cutting and assembling the townhouse given in Project 3, again cutting the pieces from 5½"-wide (14cm) poplar board and making the entrance holes 1¼" (3.2cm). Putty and sand the assembled house. Give the house two coats of Raspberry Wine, sanding between coats. When dry, transfer the windows and door with white graphite paper.

Palette

Apple Barrel acrylic colors
- Antique White
- Black
- Country Gray
- Forest Green
- Leaf Green

Ceramcoat acrylic color
- Salem Green

Flower colors of your choice

FolkArt acrylic colors
- Camel
- Clover
- Raspberry Wine

Front Door

Salem Green

Camel

Details in Black

Door lines in watery Black

Small Back Window

Black and Salem Green

Camel

Details in Black

Antique White

Large Back Window

Black and Salem Green

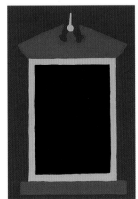
Camel

Details in Black

Antique White

2 Painting the Door and Back Windows

Fill in the windows with Black. Start the trimwork with Salem Green. Paint the door and remaining trim with Camel. Use the pattern to transfer the door details. Paint the porch light with Black. Paint the door lines with watery Black. Use white graphite paper to trace in the lines for the stoop and sidewalk. Paint these with Country Gray. Shade the step and sidewalk with watered down Black, using the same technique as you did with the curtains. Paint the curtains with watery Antique White. When dry, transfer the muntin lines with white graphite paper, then paint them in with Antique White.

3 Painting the Gingerbread, Front and Side Windows

Use the same colors as in step 2 to paint the gingerbread and remaining windows: Salem Green, Camel, Black for details and Antique White for the curtains and muntins.

Small Front Window

Black and Salem Green

Camel

Details in Black

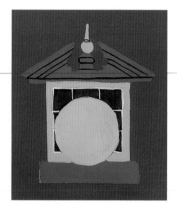

Antique White

Gingerbread Trim

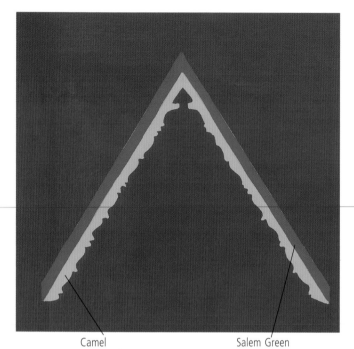

Camel   Salem Green

Side Windows

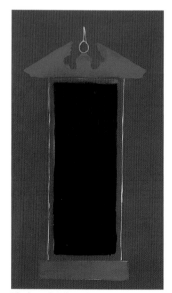

Black and Salem Green

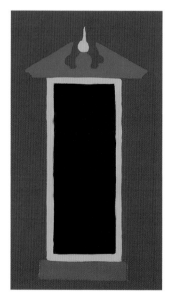

Camel

Details in Black

Antique White

Bricks

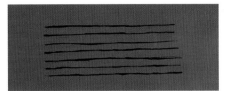

Horizontal lines

Stagger vertical lines

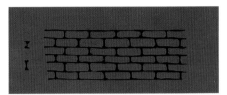

Thicken mortar

Shade with watery Black

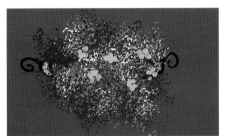

Add random touches of watery White

4 Painting the Bricks
Using a pencil, draw the horizontal lines ³⁄₁₆" (.5cm) apart, just like you did for the clapboard. Stagger the vertical lines to imitate bricks. Using watery Black, thicken the mortar and create little triangles at the top and bottom of each vertical line. Randomly shade the bricks with watery Black and White.

Greenery and Flowers

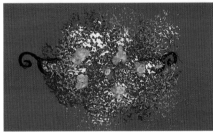

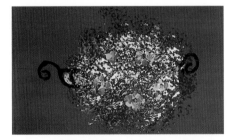

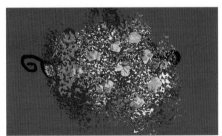

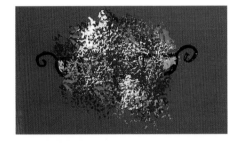

5 Painting the Greenery and Flowers
Use white graphite paper to transfer the lines for the window baskets. Paint with Black. Sponge in the greenery around the house and window boxes, using Forest Green first, then Clover, then Leaf Green and finish with a smidge of Forest Green again. Paint the bottom of the house a dark green. Sponge White over the greenery before painting the flowers. Use your own flower colors; mine are just a blotch of dark color followed by a blotch of lighter color, some made with a sponge and some with a no. 1 round brush. Sign and date your birdhouse. Add the perches—the top one is Raspberry Wine and the bottom is Camel—and polyurethane the entire house.

6 Adding the Roof and Chimney

This roof is a little larger in size because it doesn't get any shingles. It can be cut from one large shingle called a *cedar undercoarse shingle shim*, which can be purchased in a bundle of various sizes at most lumber stores. If you are only planning to make one birdhouse, it would be a waste to buy a whole bundle of these shingles, so I'd recommend choosing a different roof treatment. If you are planning to make other cedar-shingled roofs, go ahead and buy a bundle. Once you've used up all of the wide pieces, you can cut the remaining shingles into 1″ (2.5cm) pieces to use as cedar shingles, as shown in Project 6. Here I'm using my scroll saw to cut the thin end of one of these shingles into long, skinny pieces to fit around the peak of the roof. These pieces should be of random length and width.

Attach the 2″-square (5.1cm) piece of scrap wood to the inside of the roof to support the chimney. On the opposite side, make a tiny X to indicate where to nail the chimney since there will be no shingles to cover up a larger mark. You won't need to paint the underside of the roof, as you will want the natural look of the wood. Cut out the chimney and paint it Raspberry Wine. Use Black for the mortar, and Black and White for the shading. When the chimney dries, give it a coat of polyurethane. Attach the roof with glue and nails, then attach the completed chimney.

7 Cutting the Molding

There is a piece of molding that is attached to the peak of the roof after you glue on the pieces of shingle at the top. Make this from ¾″ × ¾″ (1.9cm × 1.9cm) solid oak cove molding. Here I am cutting the end in a decorative curve with my scroll saw. If you don't have the ability to cut a curved end, simply cut it straight across, or ask a friend with a scroll saw to cut a few pieces for you in case you want to use this type of roof again.

8 Painting the Molding

To hold the molding as you paint it, use a very tiny drop of hot glue to temporarily attach scraps of wood to the bottom to serve as a stand—this way you don't have to touch the wet paint or polyurethane. Basecoat the molding with Salem Green. Paint the bottom stripe with Raspberry Wine. Use white graphite paper to transfer the gingerbread details at the top. Paint the gingerbread with Camel. When dry, polyurethane the molding.

End View

 Salem Green

 Raspberry Wine

 Camel

9 Completing the Roof

Glue the shingles to the peak of the roof as shown. I added a piece of scrap wood to the peak that fits under the piece of molding. You could also use a dowel rod, or leave the peak empty. Using Liquid Nails, PC-11 or hot glue, attach the molding to the peak.

Green Townhouse
With Cedar Shake Shingles

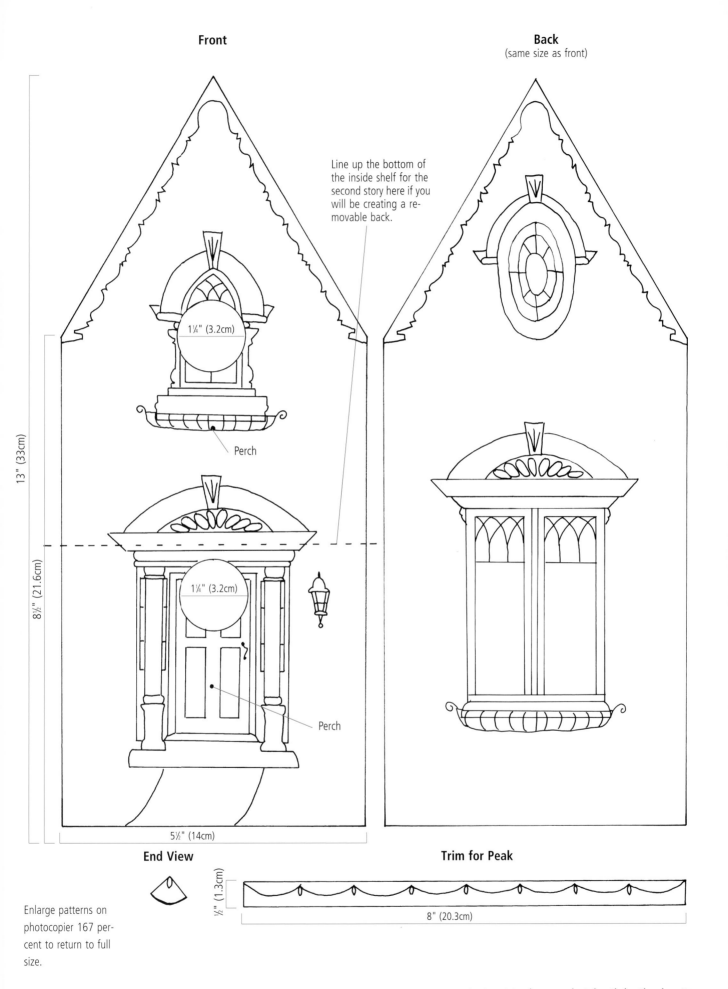

Front

Back
(same size as front)

Line up the bottom of the inside shelf for the second story here if you will be creating a removable back.

1¼" (3.2cm)

Perch

1¼" (3.2cm)

Perch

13" (33cm)

8½" (21.6cm)

5½" (14cm)

End View

Trim for Peak

½" (1.3cm)

8" (20.3cm)

Enlarge patterns on photocopier 167 percent to return to full size.

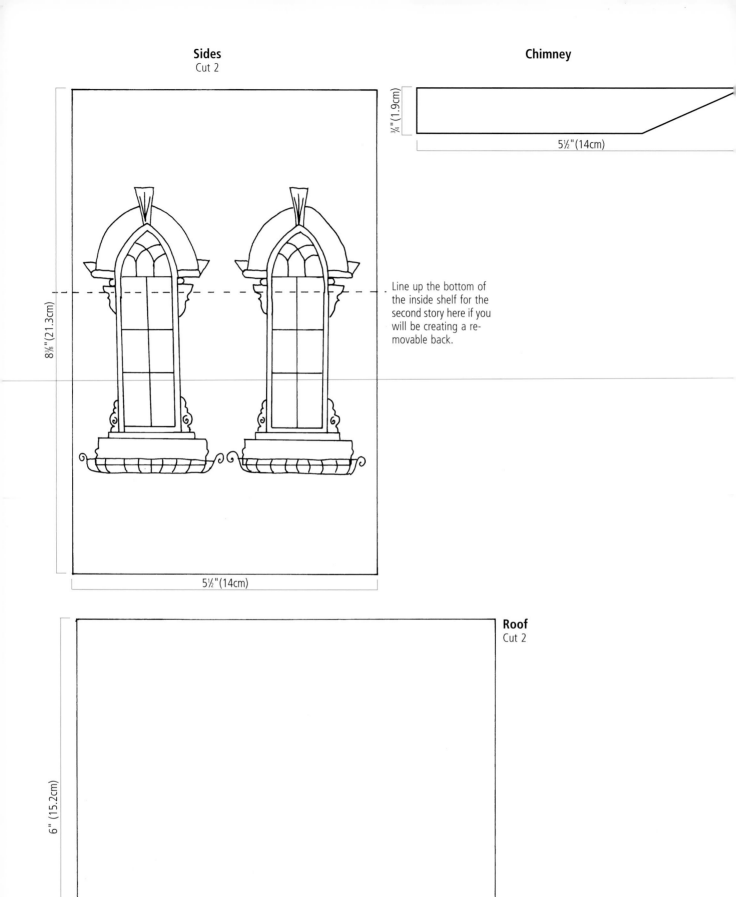

Sides
Cut 2

Chimney

¾" (1.9cm)

5½"(14cm)

8⅞"(21.3cm)

Line up the bottom of the inside shelf for the second story here if you will be creating a removable back.

5½"(14cm)

Roof
Cut 2

6" (15.2cm)

7½" (19.1cm)

Enlarge patterns on photocopier 167 percent to return to full size.

Side Windows

Black

Candy Bar Brown

English Mustard

Camel

Rose Garden

Forest Green

Antique White

1 Basecoating

Follow the instructions for cutting and assembling the townhouse given in Project 3, again cutting the pieces from 5½"-wide (14cm) poplar board and making the entrance holes 1¼" (3.2cm). Putty and sand the assembled house. Give the house two coats of Green Sea, sanding between coats. When dry, transfer the windows and door with black graphite paper.

2 Painting the Side and Large Back Windows

Paint all the windows Black. Paint the trimwork and peak as shown using Candy Bar Brown, English Mustard, Camel, Rose Garden and Forest Green. When dry, transfer the muntin lines with white graphite paper, and paint them in with Antique White. Use watery Antique White to paint the curtains.

Palette

Apple Barrel acrylic colors
- Antique White
- Black
- Country Gray
- Forest Green
- Leaf Green

Ceramcoat acrylic colors
- Candy Bar Brown
- Green Sea

FolkArt acrylic colors
- Camel
- Clover
- English Mustard
- Rose Garden

Flower colors of your choice

Large Back Window

Black and Candy Bar Brown

English Mustard

Camel and Rose Garden

Forest Green

Candy Bar Brown

English Mustard

Camel

Rose Garden

Forest Green

Watery Black linework

Black details

Antique White

Small Front Window

3 Painting the Door
Use the same colors to paint the front door, starting with Candy Bar Brown. Fill in the door with Camel, then continue the trimwork as shown. When dry, transfer the door panel lines and details with black graphite paper. Go over the panels with watery Black. Paint the porch light, doorknob and sidelights with thicker Black acrylic. Allow the paint to dry, then transfer the muntin lines onto the sidelights with white graphite paper. Go over the lines with Antique White. Paint the sidewalk and stoop with Country Gray and use very thin Black to do a little shading.

4 Painting the Small Front Window
Using the same colors, paint the front window. Transfer the muntin lines and go over them with Antique White. This window doesn't have any curtains.

Black

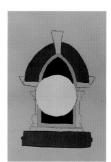

Candy Bar Brown

English Mustard

Camel

Rose Garden

Forest Green

Antique White

Oval Back Window

Black

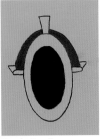

Candy Bar Brown

English Mustard

Camel

Rose Garden

Forest Green

Greenery

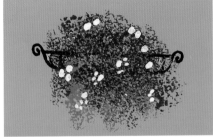

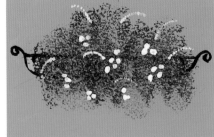

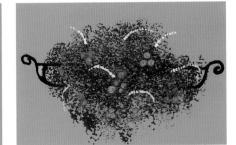

5 **Painting the Oval Back Window**
The oval back window is painted in the same way as the previous windows. After transferring and painting the muntin lines, paint one central curtain, as shown for the oval window in step 2 on page 61.

6 **Adding the Clapboard and Greenery**
Using a pencil and straightedge, draw in the lines for the clapboard siding ³⁄₁₆" (.5cm) apart. Go over the lines with very watery Forest Green. When dry, use black graphite paper to transfer the lines for the window baskets and paint them with Black paint. Fill the baskets with Camel, then sponge in the greenery around the house and window boxes, using Forest Green first, then Clover, then Leaf Green and finish with more Forest Green. Paint the bottom of the house a dark green and polyurethane it. To paint the window basket flowers, use a no. 1 round brush and White paint to make lines of dots and single circles. Add other colors over the White dots. The flowers around the base of the house are painted using a combination of sponging and round brush dots to create a variety of flower shapes, as shown.

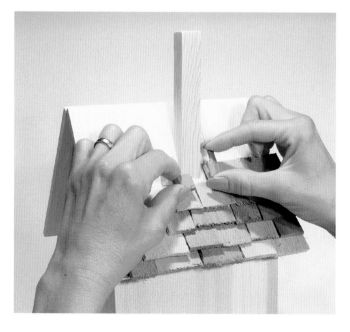

7 Finishing the House

Add the perches, painting the top one Green Sea and the bottom one English Mustard. Sign and date the house and give it one to two coats of polyurethane. Cut and assemble the roof as you did for the other townhouses, except that you will not need to paint the underside of the roof. Paint the chimney Candy Bar Brown and use Black for the mortar. Shade the bricks with watered down Black and Antique White. Polyurethane the chimney and nail it in place over the support block.

8 Cutting the Cedar Shingles

Divide a cedar shake shingle into 1" (2.5cm) strips. Using a scroll saw or hand-saw, start at the thinnest edge of the shingle and cut the strips apart, working toward the fattest end. You will get about four or five rows from each shake shingle before it becomes too thick to make good bird-house shingles. To test the thickness of your shingles, lay one strip over another. If you get a huge gap under the shingles, they are too thick.

9 Shingling the Roof

Once you have a good supply of 1" (2.5cm) strips, cut them into squares with a coping saw, or break them into pieces by hand. I lay my shingles on a piece of scrap wood to make them easier to cut. Shingling with cedar shingles is no different than roofing with Safety Walk. Start with a piece ½" (1.3cm) in width and the same length as the roof. Glue it down with hot glue and then work the rows up, staggering the lines. The shake shingles don't have to be uniform in length. I like mine to have a shaggy look. Stop shingling one row before you reach the peak.

Use a coping saw to cut specially angled pieces to fit around the chimney.

End View

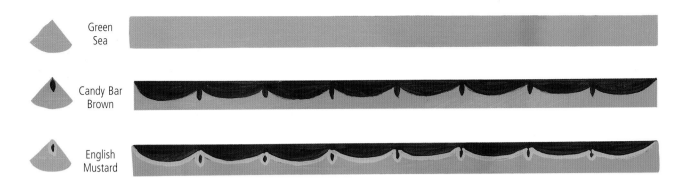

Green Sea

Candy Bar Brown

English Mustard

10 **Adding the Peak Trim**
I used a piece of ½" (1.3cm) quarter round pine for the piece at the peak of the roof. Cut it on a scroll saw to the pattern dimensions, and then sand. Give it two coats of Green Sea and allow to dry. Transfer the pattern with black graphite paper, then paint the trimwork with Candy Bar Brown and line it with English Mustard. When dry, give it a coat or two of polyurethane and glue it into the peak. Butt the last row of shingles right up to this trim.

Blue Three-Story With Tall Chimney

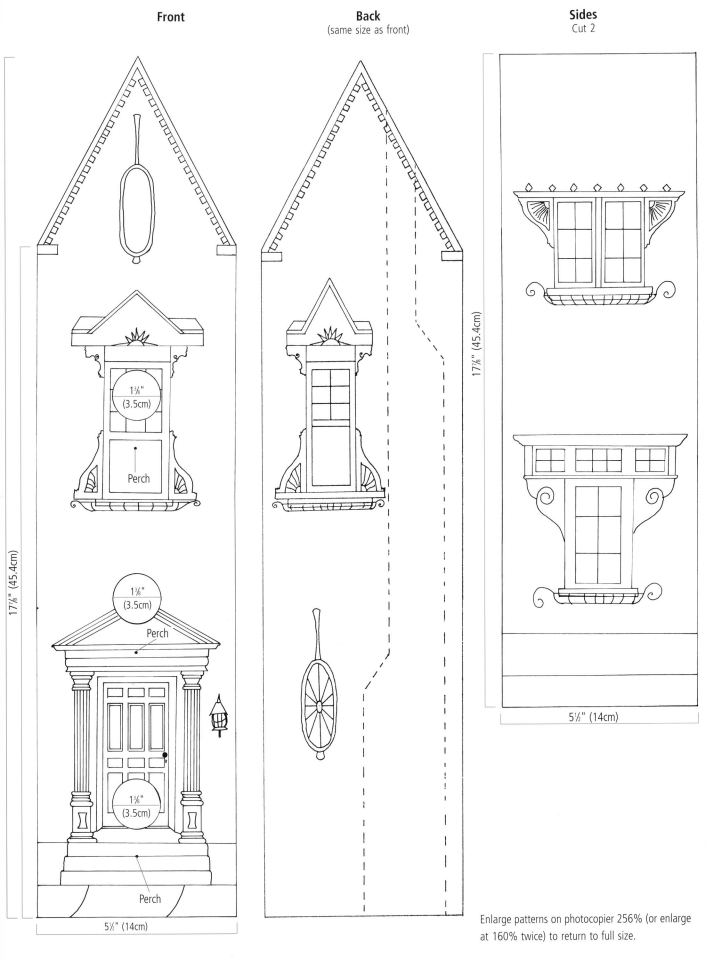

Front

17⅞" (45.4cm)

1⅜" (3.5cm)

Perch

1⅜" (3.5cm)

Perch

1⅜" (3.5cm)

Perch

5½" (14cm)

Back
(same size as front)

Sides
Cut 2

17⅞" (45.4cm)

5½" (14cm)

Enlarge patterns on photocopier 256% (or enlarge at 160% twice) to return to full size.

Project 7: Blue Three-Story With Tall Chimney 75

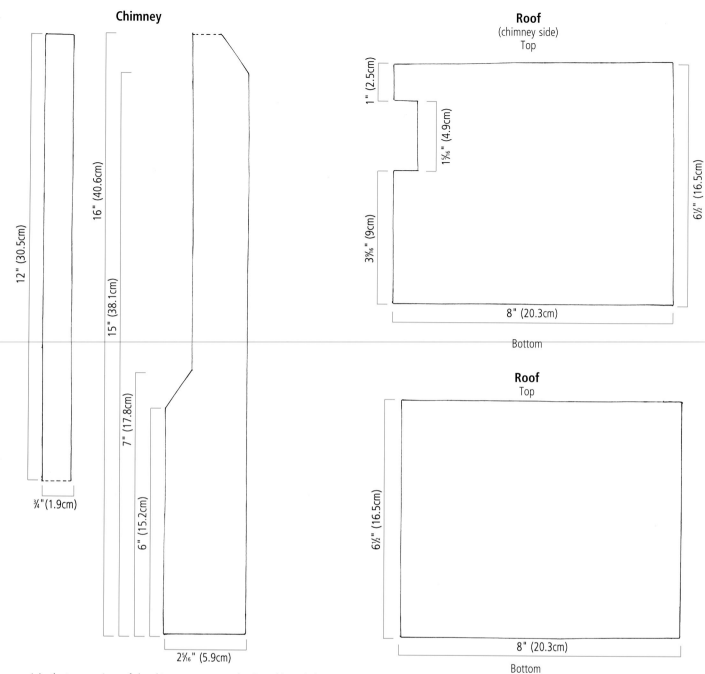

Chimney

12" (30.5cm)

16" (40.6cm)

15" (38.1cm)

7" (17.8cm)

6" (15.2cm)

¾" (1.9cm)

2⁵⁄₁₆" (5.9cm)

Roof
(chimney side)
Top

1" (2.5cm)

1⁵⁄₁₆" (4.9cm)

3⁹⁄₁₆" (9cm)

6½" (16.5cm)

8" (20.3cm)

Bottom

Roof
Top

6½" (16.5cm)

8" (20.3cm)

Bottom

Join the two sections of the chimney pattern at the dotted lines before cutting. The chimney is cut in one complete piece, 28" (71.1cm) tall.

Palette

Americana acrylic colors
• Hauser Light Green
• Russet
• True Ochre

Apple Barrel acrylic colors
• Antique White
• Black
• Country Gray
• English Ivy Green
• Territorial Beige
• Vineyard Green
• White

Ceramcoat acrylic colors
• Green Sea
• Nightfall Blue

FolkArt acrylic colors
• Coffee Bean
• Green Meadow

Flower colors of your choice

Enlarge patterns on photocopier 259 percent (or enlarge at 160 percent twice) to return to full size.

Although Projects 7, 8 and 9 are built in the same way, be sure to follow the exact pattern given for the three-story you're building—as you can see, the rooflines and hole positions vary.

Side Top Windows

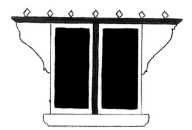

Black and Russet

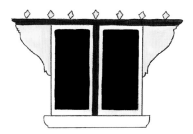

Thinned True Ochre

True Ochre

This is what the window will look like when surrounded with blue.

1 Building the Three-Story House
The three-story house is built in the same way as the two-story townhouse, using the 6″ (15.2cm) precut poplar board, which is actually 5½″ (14cm) wide. The only differences will be that you will cut two additional pieces from scrap one-by pine the same size as the base (for inner shelves) and you will drill three entrance and three perch holes. Assemble the front, sides and base. Use an all-weather glue to position the shelves inside the house, then secure them with nails. Attach the back, skipping the glue if you will be removing it for cleaning. Fill the nail holes with wood putty and sand them when dry. Give the house two coats of White paint, sanding between coats. You will complete the windows and doors, then paint around them with blue. (Starting with a dark blue base coat would require you to add layer upon layer of lighter trim colors to keep the dark background from showing.)

2 Painting the Side Top Windows
Transfer the windows and doors with black graphite paper. Fill in the windows with Black. Start the trimwork with Russet, then add a very watery mix of True Ochre as shown. This thin application of yellow over white will be much paler than the full-strength ochre lines added next. When this is dry, transfer the fanlike details onto the sides of the windows and go over these lines with undiluted True Ochre. Transfer the muntin lines with white graphite paper and paint them with Antique White. Paint in the curtains with watery Antique White.

Shortcut

If you don't have the time or desire to make an entire three-story house, just cut and paint the front piece, add two scrap pieces of wood in an upside-down V to represent the roof, and use this two-dimensional birdhouse as a decorative wall hanging. Or adapt the windows and doors to fit a smaller or ready-made birdhouse. I find it very relaxing and therapeutic to paint these big houses, even if I only paint on them a little each day.

Side Bottom Windows

Black and Russet

Thinned True Ochre

True Ochre

This is what the window will look like when surrounded with blue.

3 Painting the Side Bottom Windows

These windows are painted in the same manner as in step 2, starting with Russet, and then thinned True Ochre. There are only two lines of undiluted True Ochre.

4 Front and Back Windows

The front and back sets of windows are painted in the same way. Fill in the windows with Black. Paint the trim with Russet, then thinned True Ochre. When dry, transfer the fanlike lines to the side pieces of the rectangular windows and the sunburst at the top. Paint these details with undiluted True Ochre. Transfer the muntin lines and paint them with Antique White. Paint the curtains with thinned Antique White. Be sure to carry all lines inside the entrance holes.

Front and Back Windows

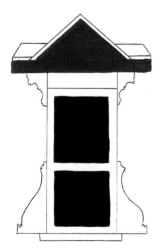

Black and Russet

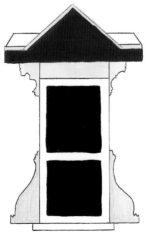

Thinned True Ochre

True Ochre

This is what the window will look like when surrounded with blue.

Black and Russet

Thinned True Ochre

True Ochre linework   Black linework

5 Painting the Front Door

Transfer all of the detail lines for the door with black graphite paper. Fill in the windows in the door with Black. Start the trimwork with Russet, then add thinned True Ochre as shown. Go over the door panels with undiluted True Ochre. Paint the doorknob and linework on the columns and lintel with Black paint. Add the curtains with watery Antique White. Paint the sidewalk and stoop with Country Gray and shade with watery Black.

6 Cutting the Chimney and Adding the Stonework

Piece the two parts of the chimney pattern together at the dotted lines. From 1″ (2.5cm) pine, cut the entire chimney in one piece. The only difference between this chimney and the chimney on the Summer Cottage is this one is taller and goes up the back in a little different position. To make painting the house and stonework easier, don't attach the chimney until you're ready to add the roof. In this picture, I've simply propped my chimney against the house so you get an idea of where it will go. Give the chimney a base coat of White, then draw in the stones freehand on the chimney and around the base of the house, making them irregular in size and spacing. Outline the stones with Black paint. Paint the area under the stonework and the base of the house Green Meadow to represent the lawn.

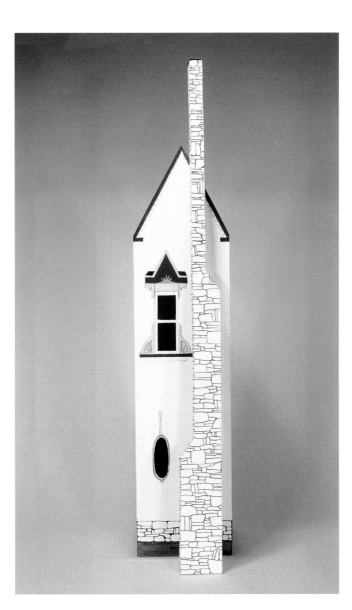

Pink Three-Story With Green Shutters

¾" (1.9cm)

7" (17.8cm)

20" (50.8cm)

13⅜" (35.2cm)

1⅜" (3.5cm)

Perch

1⅜" (3.5cm)

Perch

1⅜" (3.5cm)

Perch

5½" (14cm)

Enlarge patterns on photocopier 224 percent (or enlarge at 150 percent twice) to return to full size.

Project 8: Pink Three-Story With Green Shutters 83

Sides
Cut 2

8⅞" (35.2cm)

5½" (14cm)

Palette

Americana acrylic colors
• Deep Teal
• Dusty Rose
• Hauser Light Green

Apple Barrel acrylic colors
• Antique White
• Black
• Country Gray
• English Ivy Green
• Lavender
• Pewter Grey
• Sky Blue
• Territorial Beige
• Vineyard Green
• White

Ceramcoat acrylic colors
• Denim Blue
• Green Sea

FolkArt acrylic colors
• Apple Spice
• Georgia Peach
• Green Meadow
• Plum Chiffon
• Rose Garden
• Wintergreen

Roof
Cut 2

8" (20.3cm)

7½" (19.1cm)

Enlarge patterns on photocopier 224 percent (or enlarge at 150 percent twice) to return to full size.

Black

Deep Teal

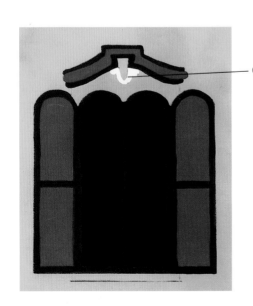

Wintergreen

Country Gray

1 Building and Basecoating the House

Using the patterns on pages 83 and 84, cut out the pieces and assemble the house as instructed in the previous project; fill the nail holes and sand. Basecoat the house with Dusty Rose.

2 Painting the Windows

Transfer the windows and door with black graphite paper. With the exception of the lower back window, shown here, the windows on this house are all the same style. All windows are painted in the following order. Paint in the window with Black. Paint the shutters and start the trim with Deep Teal, then add Wintergreen, Country Gray, Georgia Peach and Rose Garden. Use white graphite paper to transfer the lines in the shutters and paint them with watery Black. Transfer the muntin lines with white graphite paper and paint them with Antique White. Paint the curtains with watery Antique White.

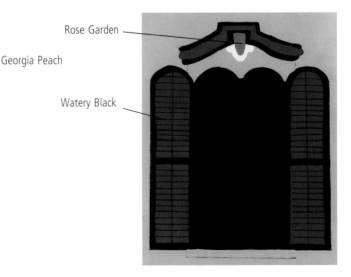

Rose Garden

Georgia Peach

Watery Black

Black

Deep Teal

Wintergreen

Country Gray

Georgia Peach

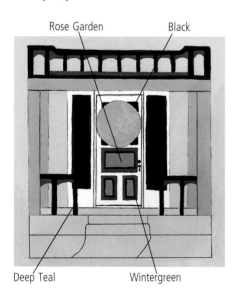

Rose Garden   Black

Deep Teal   Wintergreen

3 Painting the Front Door
The door is painted with the same sequence of colors as the windows. After filling in the door with Georgia Peach, transfer the door panels, doorknob and other detail lines with black graphite. Paint the doorknob and door lines with watery Black. Paint the center of the panels with Rose Garden, outline with Deep Teal and then go around the Deep Teal with a thicker border of Wintergreen. Transfer the muntin lines with white graphite paper and paint the muntins and curtains with Antique White. Paint the stoop and sidewalk with Country Gray and shade with watery Black.

4 The Stonework and Chimney
Basecoat the stonework area and chimney with Georgia Peach. When dry, draw in the stonework and paint the mortar between the stones with Pewter Grey. Shade the stones with watery Black. Paint the lawn area and base of the house with Green Meadow. Next add the clapboard siding lines, using a pencil and straightedge to space them ⅜" (1cm) apart. Go over the lines with thinned Rose Garden.

5 Painting the Greenery

Transfer the window baskets with black graphite paper and paint them Black; fill the insides with Territorial Beige for straw. Sponge the greenery, starting with English Ivy Green, then Vineyard Green, Hauser Light Green and finally Green Sea. The flowers in the window boxes are circles of Rose Garden and Apple Spice, loaded on the brush simultaneously. Little White dots form the white sprigs of flowers. All of the other flowers are sponged on.

6 Finishing the House

Cut three perches 1¼″ (3.2cm) long and glue them in place. Paint the top perch Dusty Rose, the middle perch Green Meadow and the bottom perch Georgia Peach. Sign and date the house and give it one to two coats of polyurethane. The roof and chimney are built in the same way as the townhouse chimneys, with the scrap block of wood added to the inside to beef up the area where the chimney will be attached. Paint the underside of the roof with two coats of Pewter Grey, and polyurethane this area as well as the chimney when dry. Glue and nail the roof and chimney in place. I added a ⅜″ (1cm) dowel rod to the peak of my roof, first painting the ends Pewter Grey. Shingle the roof with 1″ (2.5cm) pieces of gray Safety Walk as instructed in previous projects.

Gray Brick Three-Story

Front

Back
(same size as front)

Chimney

¾" (1.9cm)

6" (15.2cm)

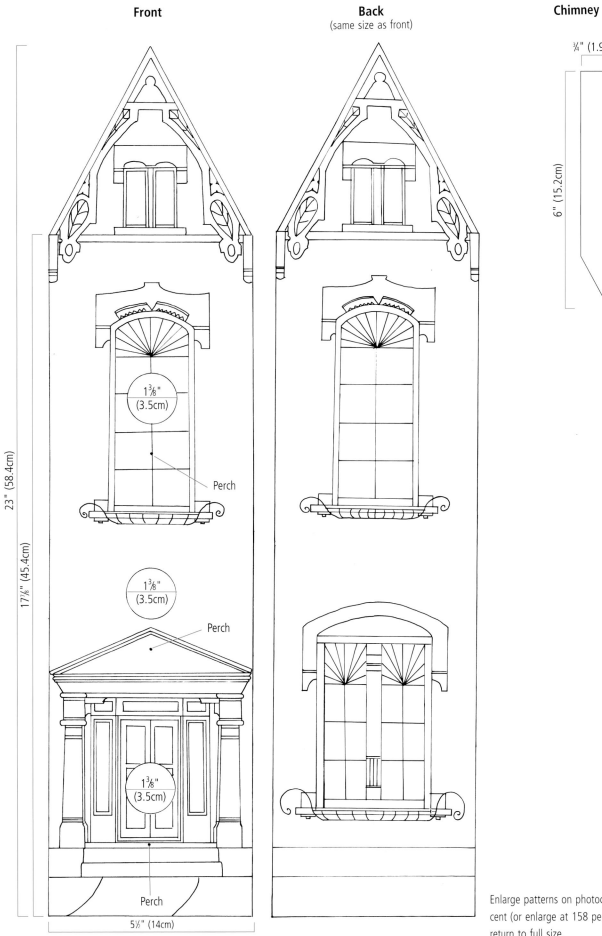

23" (58.4cm)

17⅞" (45.4cm)

1⅜"
(3.5cm)

Perch

1⅜"
(3.5cm)

Perch

1⅜"
(3.5cm)

Perch

5½" (14cm)

Enlarge patterns on photocopier 251 percent (or enlarge at 158 percent twice) to return to full size.

Sides
Cut 2

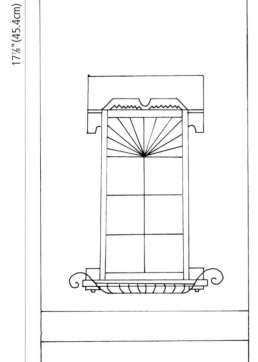

17⅞" (45.4cm)

5½" (14cm)

Palette

Americana acrylic colors
- Hauser Light Green
- Medium Flesh
- Moon Yellow
- True Ochre

Apple Barrel acrylic colors
- Antique White
- Black
- English Ivy Green
- Sky Blue
- Territorial Beige
- Vineyard Green
- White

Ceramcoat acrylic colors
- Denim Blue
- Green Sea

FolkArt acrylic colors
- Almond Parfait
- Apple Spice
- Bayberry
- Green Meadow
- Wintergreen

Roof
Cut 2

8" (20.3cm)

6½" (16.5cm)

Enlarge patterns on photocopier 251 percent (or enlarge at 158 percent twice) to return to full size.

1 Building and Basecoating the House

Using the patterns on pages 89 and 90, cut out the pieces and assemble the house as instructed in Project 7; fill in the nail holes and sand. Mix a very small amount of Black into White to get a light gray for the base coat. Mix enough to give the entire house two coats and do any touch-ups necessary. Be sure to sand between coats.

Side, Front and Top Back Windows

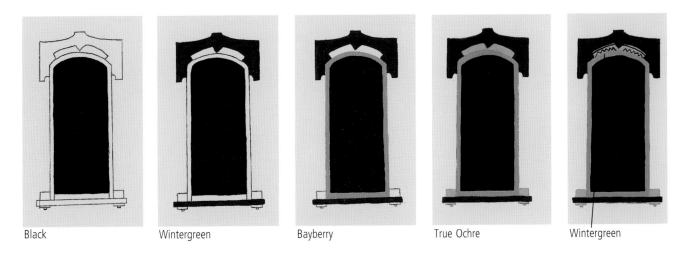

Black Wintergreen Bayberry True Ochre Wintergreen

Lower Back Window

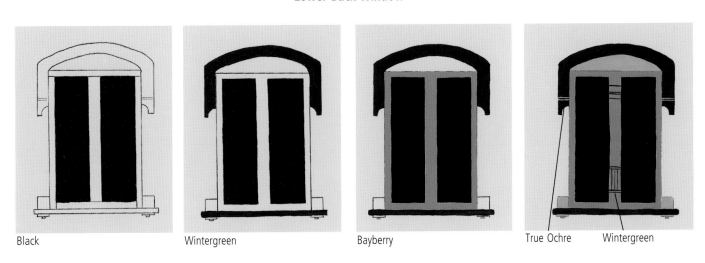

Black Wintergreen Bayberry True Ochre Wintergreen

2 Painting the Windows

All the windows on this townhouse are the same style, with the exception of the lower back window and the small window under the front eaves. All but the eave windows are painted in the following sequence: Transfer the window and door patterns with black graphite paper. Fill in all of the windows with Black. Paint the trimwork with Wintergreen, Bayberry and then True Ochre. Transfer the detail lines with black graphite paper and paint them with Wintergreen. Transfer the muntin lines with white graphite paper and paint these lines and the curtains with Antique White.

Black and Wintergreen

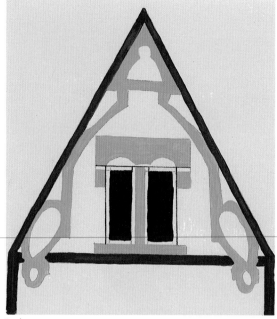

Bayberry

True Ochre

 Wintergreen

3 **Painting the Eaves and Top Front Window**
Transfer the eave pattern with black graphite paper. Fill in the window with Black. Start the trimwork with Wintergreen, then Bayberry and True Ochre. Transfer the detail lines and paint these with Wintergreen. Transfer the muntin lines with white graphite paper and paint the lines and curtains with Antique White.

Black

Wintergreen

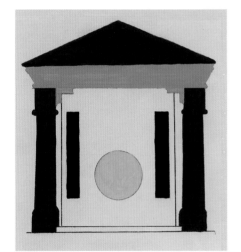

Bayberry

True Ochre

4 Painting the Front Door
Fill in the sidelights with Black. The trim is painted in the same sequence as the windows: Wintergreen, Bayberry and True Ochre. When the door is dry, transfer the detail lines with black graphite paper. Paint the panel lines and lines on the Bayberry areas with watery Wintergreen. Paint the other detail lines on the True Ochre areas with watery Black. Transfer the lines on the Wintergreen areas with white graphite paper, then paint them in with Bayberry. Shade the steps with watery Black.

White graphite lines   Watery Wintergreen

Black

Bayberry

5 Painting the Bricks

Fill in the bottom lawn area and base of the house with Green Meadow. Using a pencil and straightedge, divide the house into horizontal lines, $^3/_{16}$" (.5cm) apart. You can cut out the chimney, basecoat it with light gray and complete the brick pattern on it now as well. Use black graphite paper to transfer the lines for the window baskets. Paint the baskets and horizontal lines Black. Now draw in the vertical lines, staggering the spacing to create the look of bricks. Paint these lines Black. Shade the bricks with very watery Black paint. Fill in the window baskets with Territorial Beige.

6 **Finishing the House**
Sponge in the greenery in the window baskets and around the house using English Ivy Green, Vineyard Green, Hauser Light Green and Green Sea. Paint the flowers in the window boxes with little dots of Apple Spice; other flowers can be made with a dot of Medium Flesh surrounded by Almond Parfait petal dots. Sponge Moon Yellow and True Ochre in the flower boxes and around the base. Glue three 1¼" (3.2cm) perches in place and paint the top one Black, the middle one Wintergreen and the bottom one with your light gray mixture. Sign and date the birdhouse. Give the house and chimney one to two coats of polyurethane.

Optional Outlines

As I worked on the greenery, I decided my Bayberry areas weren't standing out enough from the light gray background. To give them more definition, I outlined all Bayberry areas with Wintergreen. You can add these outlines to your birdhouse if you think you need them.

7 **Completing the Roof**
Paint the underside and edges of the roof with Black and polyurethane these areas when dry. Add the piece of scrap wood inside the roof to support the chimney. Glue and nail the roof pieces in place, then attach the chimney. I have added a ⅜" (1cm) dowel to my roof peak, first painting the ends Black. Shingle the roof with 1" (2.5cm) squares of black Safety Walk as in previous projects.

Small Town Mercantile

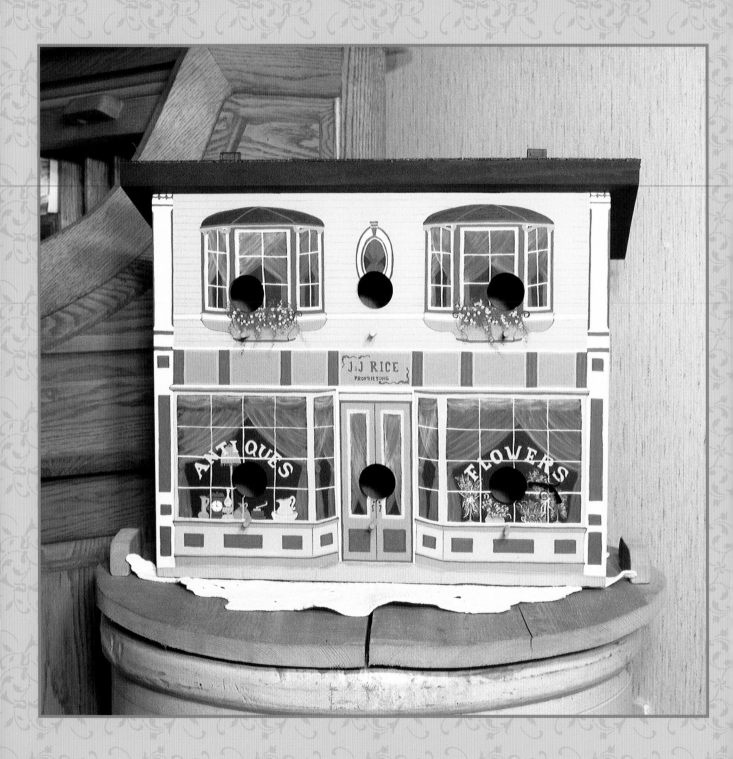

Right Side

Left Side
(same size as right)

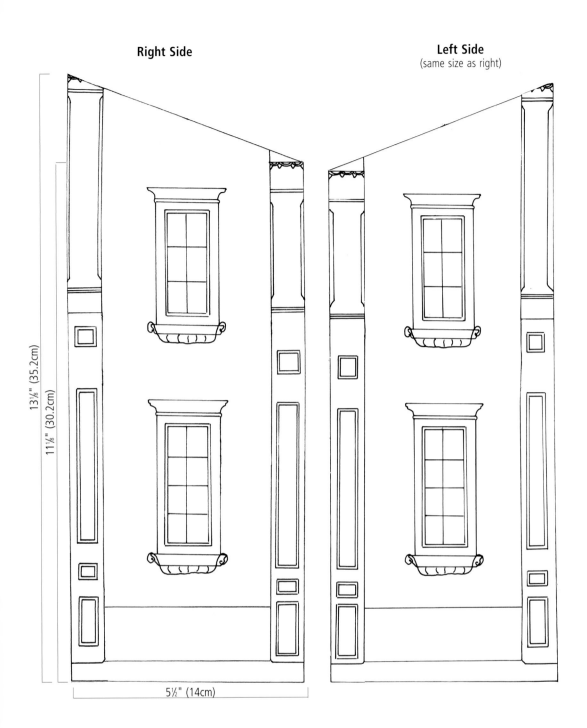

13⅛" (35.2cm)

11⅛" (30.2cm)

5½" (14cm)

Roof

9" (22.9cm)

19" (48.3cm)

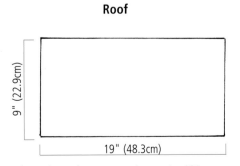

Enlarge the roof pattern on photocopier 900 percent (or 174 percent four times) to return to full size.

Chimney
Cut 2

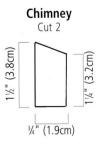

1½" (3.8cm)

1¼" (3.2cm)

¾" (1.9cm)

Enlarge patterns on photocopier 224 percent (or enlarge at 150 percent twice) to return to full size.

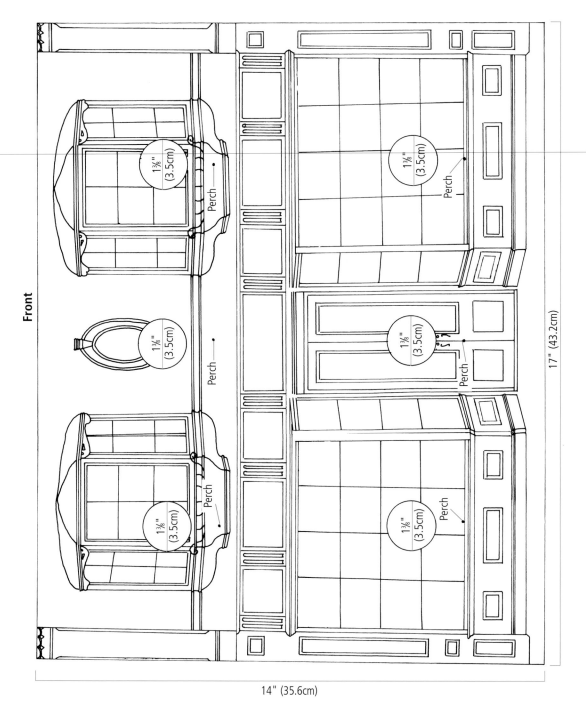

Front

1⅜" (3.5cm)

Perch

1⅜" (3.5cm)

Perch

1⅜" (3.5cm)

Perch

1⅜" (3.5cm)

Perch

1⅜" (3.5cm)

Perch

1⅜" (3.5cm)

Perch

14" (35.6cm)

17" (43.2cm)

Enlarge pattern on photocopier 224 percent (or enlarge at 150 percent twice) to return to full size.

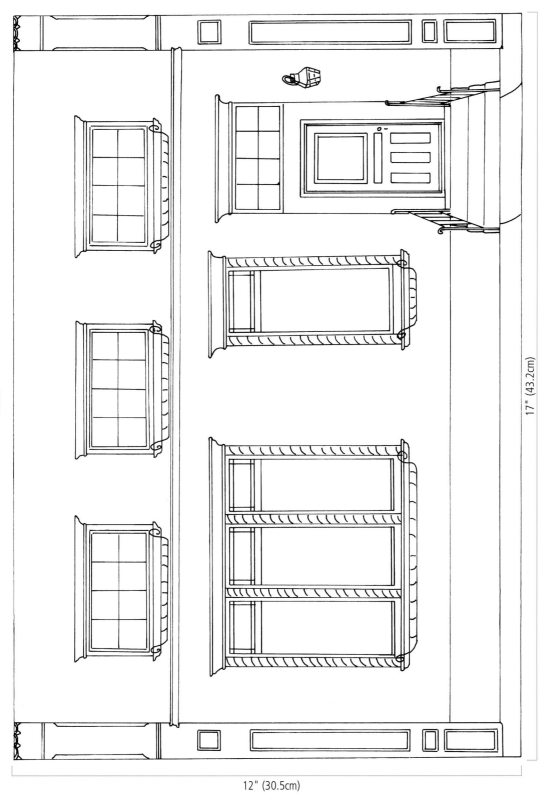

Back

17" (43.2cm)

12" (30.5cm)

Enlarge pattern on photocopier 224 percent (or enlarge at 150 percent twice) to return to full size.

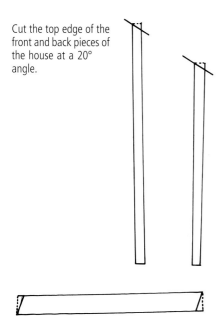

Cut the top edge of the front and back pieces of the house at a 20° angle.

Also cut the front and back edges of the roof at a 20° angle.

1 Building the Mercantile

Cut the front, back and side pieces from a piece of ½" (1.3cm) plywood, good on one side. Cut a 20° angle on the top edge of the front and back pieces using a table saw. If you aren't an experienced woodworker, you might ask someone to help you. Next cut the entrance holes and drill the perch holes. Glue and nail the front and sides together. Use the partially assembled house to determine the size of the base and cut it from a piece of 1" (2.5cm) pine. Glue and nail it in place. Cut another piece the same size as the base from a scrap of thin plywood. This will serve as the horizontal partition inside the house. Glue and nail it in place, then measure from the base to the horizontal partition. Cut two pieces of plywood this height and 5½" (14cm) in width for the bottom vertical partitions and attach. Measure from the horizontal partition to the highest point on the front piece to get the height of the top two vertical partitions. The width will again be 5½" (14cm). Cut the top edges of these two pieces to a 20° angle and glue and nail them in place. Attach the back. Fill the nail holes with wood filler and sand when dry. Basecoat the entire store with Victorian Green. When dry, transfer the patterns with black graphite paper.

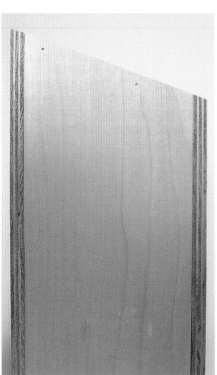

Cutting the front and back at this angle allows the roof to fit better.

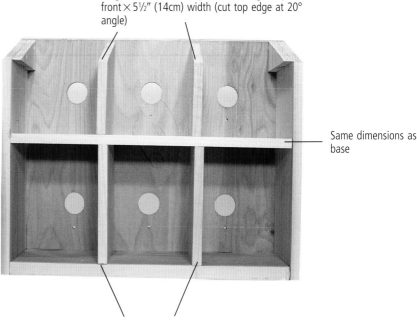

Height from horizontal partition to highest point of front × 5½" (14cm) width (cut top edge at 20° angle)

Same dimensions as base

Height from base to horizontal partition × 5½" (14cm) width

Palette

Americana acrylic colors
- Avocado
- Hauser Light Green
- Mississippi Mud
- Plantation Pine
- Plum
- Yellow Ochre

Apple Barrel acrylic colors
- Antique White
- Country Gray
- Green Meadow
- Lilac Dust
- Sage Green
- Victorian Green
- Vineyard Green

FolkArt acrylic color
- Thicket

Flower Colors of Your Choice

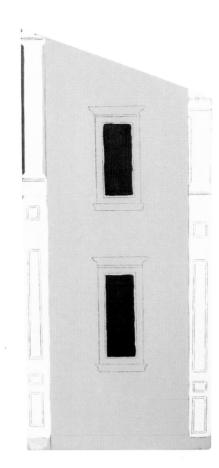

2 Painting the First Trim Color

Fill in all of the windows and tops of the bow windows with Black. Start the trimwork with Antique White as shown.

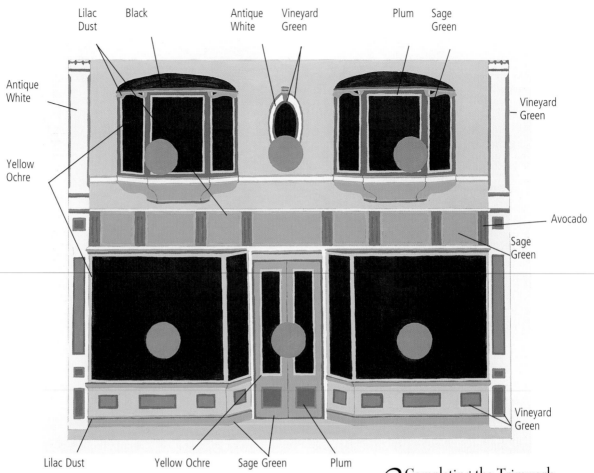

Lilac Dust · Black · Antique White · Vineyard Green · Plum · Sage Green

Antique White

Yellow Ochre

Vineyard Green

Avocado

Sage Green

Vineyard Green

Lilac Dust · Yellow Ochre · Sage Green · Plum

3 **Completing the Trimwork**
Paint the other areas of trimwork as indicated using Yellow Ochre, Avocado, Plum, Lilac Dust, Sage Green and Vineyard Green. Paint the lawn area with Green Meadow. Paint the sidewalk and steps with Country Gray and shade with very watery Black.

4 **Adding More Details**
Transfer the muntin lines and the lines on the tops of the bow windows with white graphite paper. Paint them Antique White, then add the curtains with watery Antique White. The finished curtains are shown on page 103. Transfer the flower baskets and step rails with black graphite paper and paint them Black. Add some brickwork to the sides and back of the mercantile with a straightedge and pencil. Paint the lines with watery Black. I have left the bricks Victorian Green so it looks like they were painted with the house.

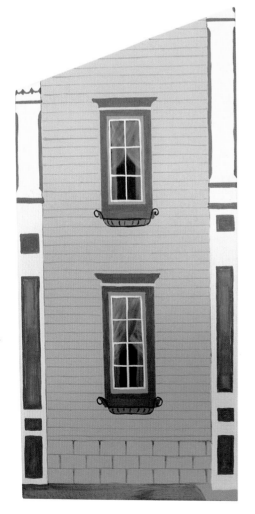

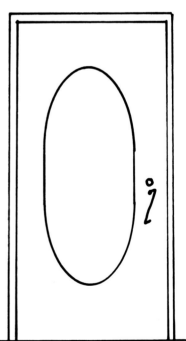

You may have noticed in the above picture that I used a different back door than the one shown in the pattern. This is the pattern for the door shown above. You can use whichever you like best.

5 Painting the Greenery and Front Windows

Paint straw in the flower baskets. Add the greenery with Plantation Pine, Thicket, Avocado and then Hauser Light Green. Sponge and paint the flowers in the colors of your choice; I used my round brush for the flowers in the boxes and the sponge for the flowers on the ground. While you have green on your palette, paint the bottom of the mercantile a dark green. Sketch your own design for the front windows on tracing paper—or use the pattern provided—then transfer the design with white graphite paper and paint accordingly. Add the perches; paint the middle one Victorian Green and all the others Sage Green. Sign and date the birdhouse and give it one to two coats of polyurethane.

When I was little, my folks shopped at a small town mercantile that sold everything you could imagine and doubled as a post office. I've always thought it would be neat to have a business like that and live above it. I'm leaving it up to you to decide what you would like your business to be. It could be a grocery, a beauty shop, a pet store, or any number of things. I chose flowers and antiques—two loves of my husband and mine. Transfer these patterns onto the front windows, or create your own.

Greenery completed on the back.

6 Roofing the Mercantile

Cut out the chimneys and paint them Plum. Draw the bricks with a straightedge and pencil. Paint the mortar and shade it with watery Black. Cut the roof from a solid piece of 1″ (2.5cm) pine. I'm using a thicker piece of wood than in previous projects because I think it looks better. Cut the front and back of the roof at a 20° angle as shown on page 100. Paint the underside of the roof Black. When dry, glue and nail the roof piece to the mercantile. Glue and nail the polyurethaned chimneys in place. Shingle the roof with 1″ (2.5cm) squares of black Safety Walk, starting with the first row at the back of the mercantile and working to the front.

Row House
on White Flower Road

Right Side
(Green)

Left Side
(Blue)

Blue House Chimney

¾" (1.9cm)

4¾" (12.1cm)

Pink House Chimney

¾" (1.9cm)

5⅛" (13cm)

Green House Chimney

¾" (1.9cm)

5⁷⁄₁₆" (13.8cm)

17⅞" (45.4cm)

5½" (14cm)

Enlarge patterns on photocopier 250 percent (or
enlarge at 158 percent twice) to return to full size.

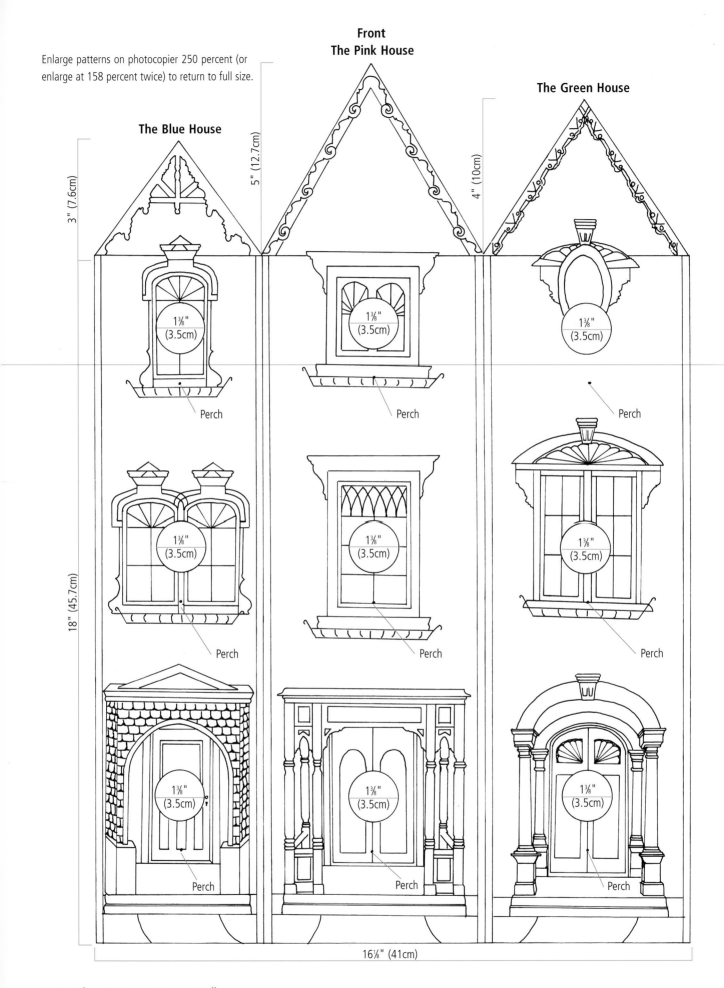

Enlarge patterns on photocopier 250 percent (or enlarge at 158 percent twice) to return to full size.

**Front
The Pink House**

The Green House

The Blue House

3" (7.6cm)

5" (12.7cm)

4" (10cm)

1⅜" (3.5cm)

1⅜" (3.5cm)

1⅜" (3.5cm)

Perch

Perch

Perch

1⅜" (3.5cm)

1⅜" (3.5cm)

1⅜" (3.5cm)

Perch

Perch

Perch

18" (45.7cm)

1⅜" (3.5cm)

1⅜" (3.5cm)

1⅜" (3.5cm)

Perch

Perch

Perch

16⅛" (41cm)

110 Making & Painting Victorian Birdhouses

The Green House

Back
The Pink House

Enlarge patterns on photocopier 250 percent (or enlarge at 158 percent twice) to return to full size.

The Blue House

4" (10cm)

5" (12.7cm)

3" (7.6cm)

18" (45.7cm)

16⅛" (41cm)

Palette

BLUE ROW HOUSE

Apple Barrel acrylic colors
- Country Tan
- Creamy Peach
- Scotch Blue
- Viking Blue

Ceramcoat acrylic color
- Green Sea

GREEN ROW HOUSE

Americana acrylic colors
- Midnite Green
- Mississippi Mud

Apple Barrel acrylic colors
- Antique White
- Wedgewood Green

Ceramcoat acrylic color
- Village Green

FolkArt acrylic colors
- Green Meadow
- Lemonade

PINK ROW HOUSE

Americana acrylic color
- Neutral Grey

FolkArt acrylic colors
- Maroon
- Potpourri Rose
- Victorian Rose

GREENERY AND STONEWORK

Americana acrylic colors
- Avocado
- Hauser Light Green
- Mississippi Mud
- Plantation Pine

Apple Barrel acrylic colors
- Antique White
- Black
- Country Gray
- Sandstone
- Vineyard Green

FolkArt acrylic colors
- Maple Syrup
- Thicket

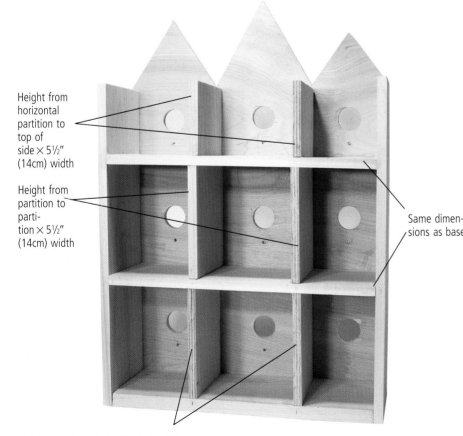

Height from horizontal partition to top of side × 5½″ (14cm) width

Height from partition to partition × 5½″ (14cm) width

Same dimensions as base

Height from base to horizontal partition × 5½″ (14cm) width

1 Building the Row House

Cut the pattern pieces from a sheet of ½″ (1.3cm) plywood, good on one side. I use a table saw to cut out the big pieces, then cut the rooflines with my scroll saw. Cut the entrance holes and drill the perch holes. Assemble the front and sides of the house in the same way as the three-story houses, using scrap pieces of wood 5½″ (14cm) wide for the inner partitions. Cut two pieces of wood the same dimensions as the base for the horizontal partitions. Then measure from the base to the bottom horizontal partition to get the height of the bottom vertical dividers, between the two horizontal partitions for the height of the middle vertical dividers, and from the top horizontal partition to the top of the sides of the house for the top vertical dividers. Glue and nail these partitions in place and attach the back. If you want to remove the back for cleaning, make a cut 1″ (2.5cm) down from the top of the back. Glue and nail the top piece in place, but attach the rest of the back with screws instead of nails and glue. Fill the holes with wood filler and sand when dry. Cut the chimney pieces and write the house color on the bottom of each with a pencil.

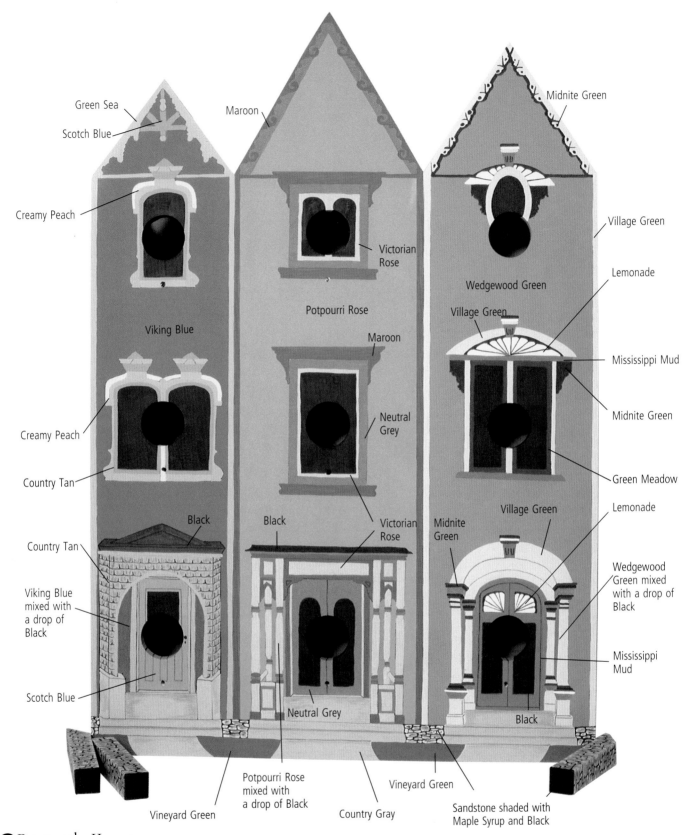

Green Sea

Scotch Blue

Creamy Peach

Viking Blue

Creamy Peach

Country Tan

Country Tan

Viking Blue mixed with a drop of Black

Scotch Blue

Vineyard Green

Maroon

Victorian Rose

Potpourri Rose

Maroon

Neutral Grey

Black

Black

Victorian Rose

Neutral Grey

Potpourri Rose mixed with a drop of Black

Country Gray

Midnite Green

Village Green

Lemonade

Wedgewood Green

Village Green

Mississippi Mud

Midnite Green

Green Meadow

Village Green

Lemonade

Wedgewood Green mixed with a drop of Black

Mississippi Mud

Midnite Green

Black

Vineyard Green

Sandstone shaded with Maple Syrup and Black

2 Painting the Houses

Painting the row house will be like painting three individual houses. First basecoat each house, allowing one color to dry before starting the next: the blue house is Viking Blue, the pink house is Potpourri Rose and the green house is Wedgewood Green. When dry, transfer the details with black graphite paper and paint the windows with Black. Paint the outer trim on the blue house with Green Sea, use Maroon on the pink house and Village Green on the green house. Complete the rest of the trimwork with the colors indicated above. Draw in the stonework on the blue house, chimneys and around the base. Paint the stone areas with Sandstone. Shade with watery washes of Maple Syrup and Black, and paint the mortar lines Black. Paint the steps and sidewalk Country Gray and shade with watery Black. Paint the lawn areas with Vineyard Green.

The back of each house is painted in the same way as the front.

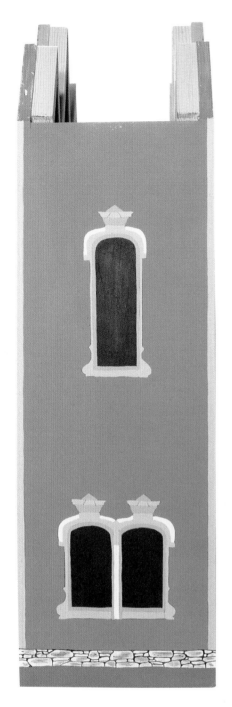

Be sure to label the bottom of each chimney so you know which house it belongs with. Paint the chimneys with Sandstone, shade them with watery Maple Syrup and Black, and detail the mortar with Black. When dry, give them one to two coats of polyurethane.

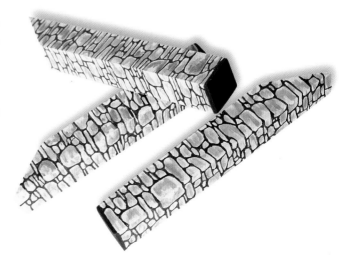

3 Adding the Curtains and Clapboard Siding

Transfer the muntin patterns with white graphite paper and paint with Antique White. Paint the curtains with watery Antique White. Draw on the lines for the clapboard siding using a straightedge and pencil. I have made the lines on the outside two houses narrower than the middle house to add variety. Paint the lines with a thinned mix of one of the darker house colors. Transfer the flower baskets with black graphite paper and paint the lines Black. Fill the insides with Mississippi Mud.

The back with windows and clapboard completed.

Right Side

Left Side

4 Painting the Greenery

Sponge in all of the greenery with Plantation Pine, Thicket, Avocado, then Hauser Light Green. I made all of the flowers with Antique White because my row house is on White Flower Road. You can make yours any color you choose. Use a combination of sponges and round brushes to create the flowers. If you haven't already done so, paint the entire bottom of the row house a dark green. Glue the perches in place and paint them the same color as the area they are in. Sign and date the house. When dry, give the whole house one to two coats of polyurethane.

The back with greenery
and flowers completed.

8½″ (21.6cm) wide   28° angle

1¼″ (3.2cm) overhang

5 Cutting and Attaching the Roofs

I cut the roof pieces from ¼″ (.6cm) poplar. You could also use plywood, good on one side. All of the roof pieces are 8½″ (21.6cm) wide. So that the three roofs fit better where they join, cut a 28° angle on the bottom edges of both roof pieces on the pink house, and on the bottom edges of the inside roof pieces on the green and blue houses. You can also leave the edges straight if you prefer. After cutting the angle, I lay the 8½″-wide (21.6cm) piece of wood in position and use a pencil to mark the proper height for the peak. I leave a 1¼″ (3.2cm) overhang at each end of the house. Sand the pieces and paint the undersides Black. Before attaching, nail a piece of scrap wood on the inside where you will be attaching each chimney. Then glue and nail the chimney in place. I attach the chimneys before the roof because it's difficult to nail between the steep roofs. Glue and nail the roof pieces in place. I've glued dowel rods, painted Black on each end, into the peaks of my roofs.

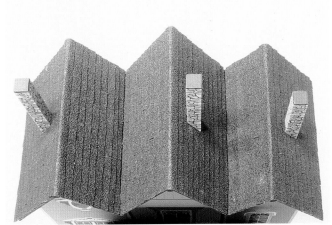

6 Shingling the Roof

I used 1″ (2.5cm) squares of black Safety Walk to shingle my roofs. First run a strip along the edges of each roof piece the width of the roof. Shingle as in the previous projects, overlapping the dowel rods at the peak with a single strip the width of the roof.

If you'd prefer a lighter roof color, use gray Safety Walk. You could also add cedar shingles, or simply paint the roof the color of your choice.

Gallery of Designs

Here are some additional patterns for doors, windows, porches and more. Mix and match these elements with the projects in this book to create a wide variety of unique birdhouses. Enlarge patterns as needed to fit your project.

Here are some elaborate windows. If you want flower baskets, trace them from other patterns.

124 *Making & Painting Victorian Birdhouses*

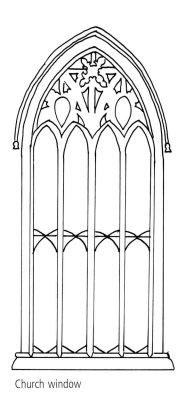

Church window

Window for a stone church

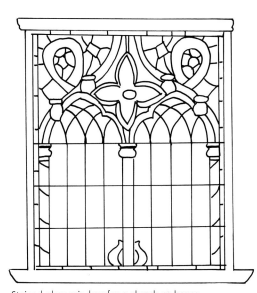

Stained glass window for a church or house

Windows for an elaborate two-story

Front steps for a church

Elaborate porches

 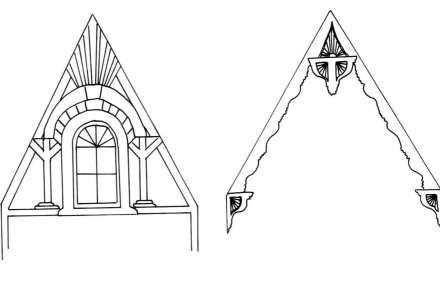

You can modify these eave trims to use on any angle of roof by tracing half of the pattern at a time.

Conclusion

It has truly been a challenge and pleasure for me to write this book. Now that I am done, I have to say it has been very rewarding. I hope you enjoyed it. I would be glad to hear from you and see pictures of the birdhouses you create. If you'd like to purchase an unfinished birdhouse like the ones I've made in this book, write to me at P.O. Box 219, Lowden, Iowa 52255 and I'll put you in contact with someone who can build it.

Index